MARCO

ROME

March 2018

CHECK FOR MAP

GERMANY
SWITZERLAND AUSTRIA
SLOVENIA
FRANCE CROATIA
SAN
MC   Florence MARINO   BOSNIA-
ITALY   HERZEG.
Corsica (F)   Rome
Sardinia (I)   Ischia   Naples
Mediterranean Sea
Milan

4/21 2X 1/15/20
C2018

www.marco-polo.com

FREE!

THE
TOURING APP

shows you the way...
including routes and offline maps!

GET MORE OUT OF YOUR MARCO POLO GUIDE

IT'S AS SIMPLE AS THIS

1 go.marco-polo.com/rom

2 download and discover

GO!

WORKS OFFLINE!

SYMBOLS

INSIDER TIP Insider-Tip

★ Highlight

🔘🔘🔘⚫ Best of …

☼ Scenic view

🌐 Responsible travel: for
ecological or fair trade
aspects

(*) Telephone numbers
that are not toll-free

**PRICE CATEGORIES
HOTELS**

Expensive over 180 euros

Moderate 110–180 euros

Budget under 110 euros

Prices are for two people
in a double room with
breakfast

**PRICE CATEGORIES
RESTAURANTS**

Expensive over 35 euros

Moderate 20–35 euros

Budget under 20 euros

Prices are for a starter
and a main course,
without drinks

DID YOU KNOW?
Spotlight on sports → p. 24
Fit in the city → p. 30
Vatican Curiosities → p. 60
Favourite eateries → p. 74
Caffè e gelato → p. 77
Time to chill → p. 88
Jazz in a tram→ p. 98
More than a good night's
sleep → p. 104
For bookworms and film
buffs → p. 109
Budgeting → p. 135
Weather → p. 136
Currency converter → p. 137

**MAPS IN THE
GUIDEBOOK**
(144 A1) Page numbers and
coordinates refer to the street
atlas and the map of Rome
and surrounding area on
p. 154/155
Coordinates are also given for
places that are not marked
on the street atlas
(0) Site/address located off
the map
Map of Forum Romanum p. 34

(*ID A–B 2–3*) refers to the
removable pull-out map

INSIDE FRONT COVER:
The best Highlights

INSIDE BACK COVER:
Plan of railway
network in Rome

The best MARCO POLO Insider Tips

Our top 15 Insider Tips

INSIDER TIP ▶ Home in Greece or Rome

Legendary frescoes, mosaics and sculptures from the apartments of Empress Livia in *Palazzo Massimo alle Terme* → **p. 38**

INSIDER TIP ▶ Last stop – gourmet bistro

At the Mercato Centrale beneath the roof-canopy of Termini railway station you will find Roman fine cuisine and the bistro owned by Michelin-star chef *Oliver Glowig* → **p. 74**

INSIDER TIP ▶ Authentic Roman cooking

Do you love Italian food? The website *www.ceneromane.com* has over 50 hosts in Rome inviting you to dinner parties in their own homes → **p. 19**

INSIDER TIP ▶ Sarcophagus dining

Did all that walking along the Via Appia Antica make you hungry? Then stop at the *Antica Hostaria L'Archeologia* garden restaurant, where fountains splash, roses bloom and the pasta is absolutely wonderful → **p. 77**

INSIDER TIP ▶ Goethe incognito

The classical German poet Goethe was an early connoisseur of Italian culture. Under the pseudonym Filippo Moeller he enthusiastically enjoyed life in the eternal city two hundred years ago. You can visit the famous traveller from Weimar in the *Casa di Goethe* → **p. 48**

INSIDER TIP ▶ Sensational panoramic vista – the National Monument

Residents of Rome refer to the bulky white *monument to King Vittorio Emanuele II* as "the typewriter". But from the top row of keys, the roof terrace at a height of 65 m/213 ft, you have a fantastic panoramic view of all periods of history → **p. 36**

INSIDER TIP ▶ Stone gossips

They may be carved in stone, but that doesn't stop the strange *statue parlanti* from talking. Once satirical verses criticising papal rulers were hung round their necks, and in the case of Pasquino the Romans still do this → **p. 126**

INSIDER TIP **Nightlife on a hill of shards**

In ancient times *Testaccio* was a rubbish tip where the Romans piled up the pottery shards of amphorae – they had no plastic or textile shopping bags. Today the *ragazzi* come here to give their all on the dance floor → **p. 92**

INSIDER TIP **Organic bistro**

Ginger is the popular meeting spot in the exclusive Via Borgognona where a hip and health-conscious clientele meet up for organic juices and teas, smoothies, soya milkshakes, salads and light pasta dishes → **p. 73**

INSIDER TIP **Glass-covered antiquity**

The 2000-year-old altar of peace, the *Ara Pacis Augustae,* is now protected by Richard Meier's ultra-modern glass roof (photo left) → **p. 48**

INSIDER TIP **Fairy houses**

The *Coppedè* quarter is like a fairy tale. The architect Gino Coppedè built wonderful villas and palazzi here in the early 20th century → **p. 66**

INSIDER TIP **Organic ice cream**

Where the ice cream tastes homemade and the fruit is delivered by organic farmers from the Piedmont or rather from the tropics: *Grom* → **p. 73**

INSIDER TIP **Original or copy?**

If you think the glossy sheen of the equestrian statue on the *Campidoglio* looks too new, you are right (photo below). Corrosive exhaust gases were too much for the original Emperor Marcus Aurelius, and he rode off to the Musei Capitolini → **p. 37**

INSIDER TIP **Picnic in the park**

Gina, a high-class snack bar on Piazza di Spagna, will make you a gourmet picnic, and all you have to do is find a nice spot in the park of Villa Borghese → **p. 77**

INSIDER TIP **The ultimate restaurant**

Housed in a former warehouse in Ostiense, the *Porto Fluviale* restaurant is the Italian equivalent of "Soul Kitchen". Their lunchtime menu is particularly delicious! → **p. 78**

BEST OF ...

FOR FREE

● *View of the Forum*

In Caesar's time Romans and travellers paid nothing to stroll across the Foro Romano. Today you have to pay for admission, but if you just want to get a glimpse, there is a view from the steps to the left of the *Campidoglio* – at its best in the evening → p. 29

● *A train to the Mediterranean*

Rome's beach fans and clubbers know the way. The almost 30-km/19-mi trip on a local train to the beach resort of *Lido di Ostia* costs only 1.50 euros, next to nothing. Lovers of archaeology take the same train and get off one stop earlier at *Ostia Antica* → p. 97

● *San Pietro through the keyhole*

The Order of the Knights of St John, whose domicile is on the Piazza dei Cavalieri di Malta, boast an unusual attraction, and so far they are not charging a fee to see the surprising view of St Peter's Basilica that you get through the keyhole of the main entrance, the *Buco di Roma* → p. 63

● *Classical music in churches*

The view of the Baroque dome of *Sant'Ignazio* is confusing. It's a painted illusion, and nothing is real. By contrast the sound of the international choirs that you can enjoy there is authentic – and the seats at the back cost nothing (photo) → p. 98

● *Monthly cultural Sunday*

On the first Sunday of every month you can visit all the national museums free of charge. And one of the world's largest museums, the *Vatican Museums,* opens its doors on the last Sunday of the month. You can also expect many other visitors on these dates → p. 36

● *Sistine chapel for free*

If you want to see the world's largest art collection, Raphael's Stanze and the Sistine Chapel without paying a penny: on the last Sunday of the month there is free admission to the *Musei Vaticani* → p. 36

⬤⬤⬤⬤⬤ Dots in guidebook refer to "Best of..." tips

● *Drink from the fountain*

Eleven aqueducts kept ancient Rome well supplied with water, and free drinking water still bubbles from numerous *fontanelle*, the little fountains in the Centro Storico. Do like the Romans do: close your hand over the spring and let the water spurt into your mouth from the upper hole → **p. 126**

● *Where politicians get their ice cream*

Rome has a dozen good ice-cream parlours, but *Gelateria Giolitti* is a must go. No matter that the prices are eye-watering and the service often rude: after heated debates nearby in parliament, Italian politicians of every party sneak off and cast their vote for one of their 40 kinds of cooling ice cream (photo) → **p. 73**

● *Step up, sit down*

Even if you've already seen a thousand photos of these gaily curving steps, the *Scalinata di Trinità dei Monti* remains one of the nicest and classiest places to sit and relax. People come here to flirt, laugh, take photos, meditate and dream the time away → **p. 53**

● *The mouth of truth*

All Romans who are newly in love make a trip to the ancient lie detector known as the *Bocca della Verità*. So far the man-sized marble face in the atrium of Santa Maria in Cosmedin has never really bitten off the hand of a beautiful woman who lied or a cynical macho – but you never know! → **p. 28**

● *Eat on the piazza*

In Trastevere there are still good ol' trattorias like *Da Augusto* on Piazza de'Renzi. There is no printed menu here, but the dishes of the day are chalked up on a blackboard by the door and everyone knows Augusto, who will come straight away with bread, water and the house wine, and take your order → **p. 79**

● *Campo de' Fiori: flower market and vanity fair*

Fewer and fewer of Rome's old market women now come to *Campo de' Fiori*, the city's most popular vegetable market, in the mornings. But this square attracts a fashionable crowd round the clock. It's a place to see and be seen → **p. 41**

ONLY IN

BEST OF ...

AND IF IT RAINS?
Activities to brighten your day

● *Galleria Alberto Sordi*
Who likes exclusive boutiques and beautiful cafés? For decades this Belle Époque building was in a dilapidated condition, but now it's a *shopping arcade* that can stand comparison with those in Milan → **p. 82**

● *MAXXimum contrast*
Rome's shockingly ultra-modern museum designed by Zaha Hadid lies between old barracks. The daring forms of this museum of contemporary art, known for short as *MAXXI*, will make you forget space and time (photo) → **p. 67**

● *Cappuccino with plaster casts*
The Romans like to drink their espresso at the counter, while the tourists prefer to sit outdoors. If it's drizzling, the *Atelier Canova Tadolini* in Via Babuini, once the studio of the sculptor Antonio Canova, is a charming place to take a *caffè* → **p. 72**

● *Down into the catacombs*
Explore miles of subterranean passages with grave niches that were hewn out of the tufa stone along the Via Appia Antica over 2000 years ago. The *catacombs* will keep you out of the rain while you examine the early history of Rome → **p. 126**

● *For chocoholics*
The trendy loft of the old *Said-Antica Fabbrica del Cioccolato* is where singles and couples come in all weathers to drink a cup of hot chocolate. If that doesn't satisfy your sweet tooth, you can buy delicious chocolate truffles by the entrance → **p. 74**

● *Tram trip with jazz concert*
Taking a trip by tram is an enjoyable way to stay dry, especially if you board the historic vehicle on a Saturday evening for a dinner with live jazz, as it rumbles from Porta Maggiore to the Colosseum, where you dine with a view of the arena → **p. 98**

RAIN

RELAX AND CHILL OUT
Take it easy and spoil yourself

● *A VIP spa for all*

At the *Benessere* spa in the five-star *De Russie* hotel you can relax cheek-by-jowl with Roman celebrities. There's a seawater jacuzzi, sauna and shiatsu treatments for the stars and normal mortals → **p. 88**

● *Laid-back Roman atmosphere*

An ideal mix between coffee house and Roman bar: Join the stylish Roman crowd gathered at the *Enoteca Il Piccolo* for an evening drink → **p. 94**

● *Relax for a midday break*

After all the sightseeing, something sensual might be tempting. Spoil yourself at the *Acanto Day Spa* with a 30-minute steam bath, an oriental snack and green tea. A nice time from 55 euros → **p. 88**

● *Surf the book bar*

Book bars like *Emporio alla Pace* are all the rage. So when in Rome, do as the Romans do and spend the morning sprawling in an armchair with a cappuccino and a newspaper, or surf the net all day long, and chill out in the evening with an aperitif and a few light bites to eat → **p. 19**

● *Swim in the Eternal City*

Although the ancient Romans had a sophisticated culture of bathing, and architecture to match, today swimming baths are thin on the ground and over-priced. If you can't afford a dip in an exclusive pool in a luxury hotel, from June to September you can make your way to the *Piscina delle Rose* and also use the spa facilities while you are there → **p. 67**

CHILL OUT

● *A wonderful piazza*

Footsore? Then treat yourself to a *latte macchiato* with a view in one of the many cafés on *Piazza Navona*, which is a square for wealthy show-offs and poor artists, for people trading and strolling, a stage for activities that the river gods on Bernini's Fountain of Four Rivers have watched impassively for centuries (photo) → **p. 45**

INTRODUCTION

DISCOVER ROME!

A colossal cinema! You leave the dark, slightly scruffy Metro B tunnel by climbing the steps, and pushing past the turnstile you are bathed in bright daylight. Suddenly, it's in front of you: the compact, four-storey wall of the Colosseum. It's so close, you can almost touch it! Even if history wasn't your favourite school subject, the presence of the almost 2000-year-old stone amphitheatre, where thousands of gladiators and wild animals were slaughtered at the signal of the Roman Emperor, makes you shudder today.

Relax and walk past the Colosseum across the wide Via dei Fori Imperiali to Piazza Venezia. On foot, by bus, by bicycle or by Segway, you find yourself immersed in history again. Follow the *footpaths of Caesar and Cicero* who once walked to their Senate office at the Forum Romanum. On summer evenings, the ruins of the government buildings of ancient Rome are magically illuminated, and perhaps you can hear the *musical strains of a rock concert* floating on the breeze from Circus Maximus. The grand and wild chariot races were held here like in the Hollywood film "Ben Hur". And as for the modern version of HP-racing: large sections of the Via dei Fori Imperiali are closed to road traffic.

Romans love to take an evening stroll past this historic site and to dive into the backstreets of the *hip nightlife quarter, Monti*, which is situated behind the pillars of the Forum of Augustus. They like to eat a crispy pizza in the open air, or chillax in a *green bar* like Aromaticus with vegan snacks, or to sample *gelato al limone* at one of the amazing ice cream stores. Everything is close to hand in Rome – the sublime and the trivial, beautiful souvenirs as well as rip-offs, 3000 years of proud history, antique marble and occasionally the odour of rubbish on street corners.

The Piazza presents a colourful parade of Roman life

Chic, flat sandals or walking shoes? The rugged Roman cobblestones are *not suitable for high heels or towering wedge shoes*. Sightseeing in Rome is worthwhile on foot. Discover *"La grande Bellezza"*, the Oscar-winning Italian cult film – and Rome's wonderfully decadent beauty. You will see that on every Piazza. This was always a substitute for Roman living rooms, as many young people live in apartments on the outskirts or still live at home with *mamma* or the mother-in-law because they can no longer afford the rents in the historic centre. The Piazza presents a colourful parade of Roman life: the market, fun fair, café bar and news stand, space

The giant rotunda of the Pantheon: a pinnacle of classical architecture

to flirt, a showcase of good taste and vanity on the scale of Circus Maximus. Here, Italians can enjoy one of their favourite pastimes and show off their *bella figura*. That's a Roman way of being ultra-cool: stepping out with inimitable elegance aside from the ordinary routine and, just for fun, making eyes at pretty tourists!

> **Pope Francis, the new attraction in the Vatican**

Find the Piazza that you like best. The largest, most ceremonial and *most photographed Piazza is naturally St. Peter's Square* – and Pope Francis is the new attraction in the Vatican. When the Argentinian pontiff appears on the balcony at Easter and Christmas for his festive blessing – the *urbi et orbi,* or "to the City and to the World" – or after a general audience joyfully drives across St Peter's Square in the popemobile, even those who aren't so religious feel inspired by the uplifting atmosphere. For the Holy Year 2016, *20 million pilgrims* alone passed through the Holy Door, which is only opened every 25 years, and otherwise remains closed.

Incidentally, *Piazza Navona, now buzzing with elegant street cafés*, was a Papal legacy. This impressive architecture and its elongated, enclosed form is fun-loving, colourful and plays on the emotions. Pope

Innocent X bestowed on his beloved sister-in-law Olimpia not only the Palazzo Pamphilj, today the seat of the Brazilian Embassy, but also spread the entire Piazza Navona at her feet. It was laid out on the site of the ruins of an *antique Roman games arena*. Patrician aristocrats and church dignitaries continued the antique contests during the 17th century. The Pope's mistress also cheered on the games from her palace windows. Where you can drink coffee nowadays, horse riders raced around the circuit like in the Palio in Sienna, bull fights raged as per the classical model and the Piazza was flooded with water for naval battles with miniature ships. Donna Olimpia not only had the favour of her Pope, but also exceptionally good taste. It was thanks to her that the Baroque genius Gianlorenzo Bernini was commissioned to build the elegant Fountain of Four Rivers. Treat yourself to several moments in front of the Piazza's magnificent babbling fountain. Every evening this is the place for *a veritable stage of street artists, portrait*

artists, tarot card readers or gold-painted mime artists who stand motionless like a statue at the centre of the vibrant street scene.

At night-time on the Piazza della Rotonda, in front of the Pantheon, Rome's beautiful people meet up – stars, A-listers and minor celebrities as well as politicians dressed in a black shirt and white summer linens – to enjoy an *aperitivo* and continue the evening in the pricey restaurants. The *ragazzi* from the suburbs prefer to buy *tramezzini* and *panini* sandwiches in the Via del Seminario and sit in front of Rome's oldest temple, according to the inscription, built by Consul Agrippa in the days of Emperor Augustus. In fact, only the inscription is authentic. The monument with the dome, which graces the space in front, was erected 100 years later. But what are a few more years compared with almost 2000 years of amazing ancient ruins?

Evening rendezvous at Campo de' Fiori

Perhaps you will be attracted more by the *Campo de' Fiori, Rome's colourful fruit and vegetable market*, which has a growing number of fashion stands. There are also *fiori* (flowers) here, though the fragrance of oranges and lemons and the smell of fish and sea food dominates. In the evenings when the market has been cleared away, orange-coloured aperitifs fill the glasses, and at sunset, people meet in the surrounding small streets to enjoy a Campari or Aperol Spritz, which Milan-based spirits company Cinzano, also known as the Campari group, is especially pleased about. You can also enjoy the cafes and restaurants in the backstreets around Campo de' Fiori.

Rome's biggest village, Trastevere, on the other side of the Tiber, is worth a visit not only to one of the *Trattoria* or to enjoy the nightlife. Although Trastevere lost some of its raw charm thanks to its redevelopment, you can still find plenty of Romantic spots with babbling fountains, tabby cats outstretched on top of walls to take their Siesta or in rubbish bins, as well as old Romans sitting in front of their houses in gowns and slippers and chatting on long summer nights. Otherwise, the former worker's quarter is buzzing with young entrepreneurs who have renovated their miniature apartments and still cultivate a Roman lifestyle. Every morning, even with iPads, they buy a newspaper from the newsstand; they only drink their espresso at the local *barista* and don't go shopping in the supermarket, but at the small *alimentari* or at the food market at Piazza S. Cosimato.

And *where are the favourite spots for Rome's clergy*? Just behind the Pantheon in the Via SantaChiara, in-between the ivy-covered Piazza dei Caprettari and the Piazza di Minerva, where a small elephant created by the Baroque sculptor Bernini bears the weight of an obelisk that is far too heavy. This is where the clergy have a fashion showroom with everything to please religious personalities – *from purple-coloured Bishop's robes to discreet grey underwear for nuns* as well as flattering jackets with a discreet pocket for a mobile phone. "Over 200 years at your service" is the motto of Annibale Gammarelli, tailor to the Vatican in the Via Santa Chiara. Pope Francis has his cassocks made here, but Gammarelli also visits the busy Pope in the Vatican.

Modern influences find it difficult to compete with so many traditions. Where one Baroque Palazzo follows the next, and where centuries-old marble, rubble and glass fragments are everywhere, avant-garde buildings must first prove their merit against Bernini's colonnades on St Peter's Square or even the Colosseum. But the *MAXXI, Zaha Hadid's revolutionary Museum of Arts of the 21st century*, has achieved this, as it floats like a summer cloud over the former barracks site in the Flaminio district. Like the futuristic Parco della Musica Auditorium by Renzo Piano, which wasn't taken seriously at first, and now attracts music lovers from around the world, Romans have even accepted the glazed canopy of the altar of peace commissioned by Emperor Augustus. The American star architect, Richard Meier, designed this. However, that doesn't necessarily mean the locals wholeheartedly endorse it.

Rowing in the Park of Villa Borghese, Rome's green oasis, can be very romantic

One Piazza in Rome wins deep affection – it cannot be missed, even though the square is small, inconspicuous and overcrowded. This is the source *probably of Italy's most famous fountain, Fontana di Trevi*, with water flowing into a broad, flat basin. From dawn until late at night people flock with delighted faces to the spray from the Baroque fountain. Is this because of the mythical attraction of the film, *La dolce vita,* when Marcello Mastroianni and Anita Ekberg jump into the gushing water on a cold night in February? Or the custom of throwing a coin into the fountain to be born again? You can find out!

WHAT'S HOT

1 Cycling alla romana

Ciclisti "A bicycle made for the seven hills" is the advertising slogan for electric bikes that are available to hire from the company Ecovia. The agile Vespa scooter is and remains the Romans' preferred vehicle and toy, although it adds to air pollution. Cycling has sporting appeal, but for many Romans a tour of the seven hills riding up- and downhill has so far proved too challenging.

The e-bike gets you mobile and no sweat – whether it's a trip to the office, market or excursion to the surrounding countryside.

Rome has certainly caught up with other European (bicycle) metropolises. Now there are bike paths running along the Tiber, *bikesharing (www. bikesharing.roma.it)* and bike hire (see p. 132). Main thoroughfares like the Via dei Fori Imperiali or Via Appia Antica are becoming traffic-free zones especially on Sundays and public holidays. Cycling route maps are available at *www.romainbici.it*.

Lowbrow art

Everyday culture and anti-culture The latest trend on the art scene in Rome aims to make art accessible for everyone, without gallery owners turning up their noses. Lowbrow – the term can be meant pejoratively and imply "bad taste". It emerged as a worldwide underground art movement inspired by comics, punk culture and other subcultures. In addition to digital art and sculptures, lowbrow artworks are printed on T-shirts and toys. To see work in the style of Pop Surrealism, go to the *Dorothy Circus Gallery (Via dei Pettinari 76 | www.dorothycircus gallery.com)* run by Alexandra Mazzanti and Jonathan Pannacciò. Artists who work in this genre include Mauro Sgarbi *(www.mauro sgarbi.com)* and Ania Tomicka *(www.ania tomicka.com)*, whose illustrations are displayed in the *Mondo Bizzarro Gallery (Via degli Equi 18A)* and elsewhere.

There are lots of new things to discover in Rome. A few of the most interesting are listed below

Guest-friendly Romans

Cene romane   Are you looking for that authentic Roman atmosphere? The latest trend to hit Rome is the intimate home-restaurant experience with over 50 Romans inviting guests to dine (from 30 euros a head) and feel at home at their houses. The Internet platform INSIDER TIP *www.ceneromane.com* coordinates the dinner parties and guests are invited to rate the intercultural experience afterwards. You can also hang out in one of Rome's literature cafes such as the *Libreria Caffè Bohemien (Via degli Zingari 36)*. In the ● *Emporio alla Pace (Via della Pace 28 | www.lemporioallapace.com)* young Romans arrive in the morning, take a seat with their laptops in one of the cafe's comfy sofas, read newspapers, eat a snack or salad for lunch and stay until late in the evening for a Mojito or glass of rosé.

Scents and sensibility

The world of perfume   L'Olfattorio Bar à Parfums (Via Ripetta, www.olfattorio.it) looks like a modern bar, but instead of a cocktail they will mix you a perfume. Roses, musk, sandalwood – sniff your way through some 200 samples and at the end you can combine them to make your very own personal scent. Rome's first perfume gallery is called *Campomarzio70 (Via di Campo Marzio 70, www.campomarzio70.it) (photo)*. Here you can book a workshop to learn the art of creating perfume. If your nose prefers something more natural, follow it to the scent garden of *L'Orto Botanico di Roma (Largo Cristina di Svezia 24)*. This 30-acre botanical garden is a delight for all the senses.

IN A NUTSHELL

B RIDAL COUPLES AT THE CAPITOL

"Where do we want to spend the happiest moment of our lives?" is the question posed by many couples. Roman bridal couples used to say, "I do" in one of Rome's many churches. Today, most prefer a civil ceremony or *matrimonio civile*, especially since Rome's most popular Registry Office is in the Palazzo Senatorio at the Capitol, one of the most magical places in the world. Stars and politicians also get married here, often for the second time.

In 2016, the Mayor Virginia Raggi celebrated the first gay wedding between the Turkish film director Ferzan Özpetek and his Italian partner, after the Italian parliament approved same-sex civil weddings.

It's a wonderful moment for photographers and onlookers: when the happy couples are married, and steal a kiss under the raised hand of Roman Emperor Marcus Aurelius. The authentic statue is next door in the Musei Capitolini, but the bronze copy is photogenic, too.

C IAO, BAMBINI

Where is all the laughter and shouting in backyards that was once as much a part of life in Rome as Vespa scooters, fountains and *gelato al limone?* The days when babies were changed during the mass on the seats in church have passed. The clergy is aware of this: "Romans, be fruitful and multiply. Have more children!" This appeal went out from Camillo Ruini,

Viva Roma – some background on the passions and peculiarities of the city and its residents

now the Emeritus Cardinal Vicar of Rome, some years ago. The retort of a Green politician was that the cardinal was like a blind man speaking about colours. However, Don Camillo did have eyes to see, and it was obvious that in his prominent diocese there were more cats than kids playing in the back yards, that the lines of washing across alleyways were not hung with children's clothes, and that elderly *signoras* were showing off fur coats rather than grandchildren when they went for a walk. Italy is regarded as a child-friendly coun-

try, but it has one of the lowest birth rates in the world, and within Italy Rome, with a mere 1.1 births per woman of child-bearing age, is way down the rankings. Even though a *mamma* with five *bambini* at the hand remains a model in Italian society, in practice many young couples are reluctant to have more than one child. The mundane reason for this is a striking lack of infrastructure. Child allowances, leave from work for parents, loans for families and tax breaks for those who have children are a distant dream. The same applies to good playgrounds, well-organised school sports or crèches and nursery schools. Only five per cent of children under three get a place in a nursery school. And the *nonna,* the grandmother who once lovingly gathered all the *bambini* to her skirts, isn't what she used to be: she goes out to work herself and has passed on her old job of child-minder to the tablet or smartphone.

FENDI: FROM LUXURY LABEL TO AN ORGANIC FARM

Every Italian knows the luxury fur-fashion house of Fendi which is why Ilaria Venturini Fendi, the granddaughter of the founders of this famous fashion house dynasty, surprises many being an organic farmer and recycling fashion designer. Her grandmother Adele founded a fur and leather shop in Rome in 1918 which

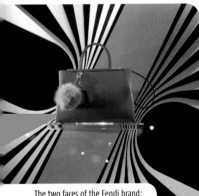

The two faces of the Fendi brand: alta moda and recycling style

her five daughters have transformed into the worldwide brand Fendi. In the nineties, the *alta moda* suffered a crisis in the luxury segment as a result of mass production and counterfeit products. Granddaughter Ilaria, who had by then joined the family company, suffered personally when militant animal-rights activists sprayed the fashion company's fur coats red or destroyed entire collections made from valuable materials such as furs and leather. She left the company in 2006 and founded her own recycling brand ⊙ *Carmina Campus* (Latin meaning "odes to the fields"). The company's name is no coincidence as Ilaria is also an organic farmer producing her own organic Pecorino cheese with milk from her happy goats on her estate outside Rome. Many of the cool eco handbags made from old safari tents, mosquito nets, umbrellas and rubbish bags or jewellery accessories from coke cans and sheet metal are manufactured by a UN women's organization in Kenya. Even former First Lady Michelle Obama bought a unique purple handbag with the eco statement "Water is Life" available from the ⊙ *Re(f)use* boutique located directly opposite the Fendi luxury temple on the Largo Goldoni *(www.carminacampus.com, www.fendi.com).*

FONTANA DI EURO

It is the dream of every European minister of finance to possess such a source of money, one that even flows in times of crisis: the Trevi Fountain. Every year, Caritas helpers fish 35,000 kg/ 77,000 lbs worth of coins (often more than 900,000 euros) out of Rome's most beloved baroque fountain. Chances are high that more millions of euros will be reached, as the city of Rome has made it illegal to fish the fountain dry and declared it a crime. This money can however only be used for humanitarian purposes and not to fill holes in the tax budget.

LA MAMMA

Behind every fictional detective *(commissario),* politician, taxi driver or *mafioso* there is a *mamma* who looks after him his whole life long: "We Italians are all *mammoni,* mother's boys", says Romano, an athletic-looking, grey-haired colonel in the Italian army. "When things are difficult or I don't like what my wife is cooking, I go home to *mamma* straight away. She understands me. Always!"

Of course the stereotype figure of the "mother hen" surrounded by her numerous brood has become rare in Rome as elsewhere, but the cult of *mamma* is stronger than ever. Because, in contrast to the situation in northern Europe, it's not a matter of chocolates and flowers once a year on Mother's Day, but of seeing *mamma* as the hub of daily existence. "The bond between a mother and her son is a life-long relationship, and daughters-in-law can only get in the way", explains a family therapist from Rome. She ought to know – her husband is a real *mammone.*

OBELISKS IN ROME?

Today tourists come back from Venice with models of gondolas, and from Paris with the Eiffel Tower. In the Caesars' days, however, one of the pencil-like, massive stone obelisks that the ancient Egyptians erected to honour their sun gods was the must-have trophy for a Roman general. Rome's most beautiful squares are adorned by twelve of them. The first was brought from Heliopolis by Augustus, and the last was looted from Axum in Ethiopia by Benito Mussolini in 1937 to add splendour to his residence, Villa Torlonia; it was returned spectacularly in 2004. If you should decide to go in search of these status symbols of the ancient world, you will be taking a tour of the best addresses in the city: they stand in front of St Peter's, the parliament and the Pantheon, on Piazza Navona and Piazza del Popolo, in front of the Quirinal Palace, the church of Santa Maria Maggiore and the Baths of Diocletian, high

Obelisks: stony souvenirs of ancient times

above the Spanish Steps and hidden away in the park of Villa Celimontana.

PAPAGALLI & PAPARAZZI

The dictionary will tell you that *papagallo* has three different meanings: a) parrot, b) pot for urinating, c) pestering admirer. In the 1960s the last of these three gained something like VIP status in Rome, when every pretty blonde or blue-eyed northern girl wanted to find out for herself whether what the magazines wrote was really true: that passionate *latin lovers* awaited them by the Spanish Steps, softly breathing "ciao bella" and "ti amo" as they offered to show visiting beauties around one of the world's most seductive cities. Perhaps the *papagalli* deserve medals for their services to European unity: many a handsome *ragazzo* of those days is still attached to his blonde *amore*.

Papagalli and *paparazzi* – hunters of skirts and celebrities – actually have little in common, except that they are both products of Federico Fellini's imagination. In the film *"La dolce vita"* the journalist Marcello (Mastroianni at his best) and his photographer, a man named Paparazzo, get into all sorts of trouble on Via Veneto – usually on the receiving end of US movie star Lex Barker's fists. This gave birth to the term "paparazzo" for a tabloid photographer. To this day the *paparazzi* and *papagalli* remain hot on the trail of celebrity snaps and pretty female tourists.

POPE FRANCIS

A more modest kind of leader: wearing the metal crucifix around his neck, his scruffy black shoes and a white skull cap on his wind-blown hair, Francis is a Pope of flesh and blood. Believers flock to St Peter's Square and love how he spontaneously embraces the old and sick or even offers to take an unknown priest or two eleven-year old students on a tour in his open-top popemobile.

Following the surprising resignation of Pope Benedict XVI, the Argentinean Jorge Maria Bergoglio was elected to the papacy on March 13, 2013. This former Archbishop of Buenos Aires has since then caused quite a stir in the Catholic Church. Following in similar footsteps to St Francis of Assisi, he calls for a "church of mercy", especially a "poor Church for the poor". Over 80 years old, he still enjoys walking places and if he is chauffeured, he prefers the old medium sized car rather than the luxury limousine! This "world priest" takes the words mercy and charity seriously and spontaneously visited the African refugees who landed on the island of Lampedusa.

In his first year, Francis tackled head on the issues of corruption and money laundering within the Vatican Bank and asked victims of clerical sex abuse for forgiveness. At the event dubbed the "Four Pope Day" held at the end of April 2014,

SPOTLIGHT ON SPORTS

What do Italian men get passionate about nowadays? The right answer is: football and football again. For a long time the king was Francesco Totti, captain of AS Roma. Scandals and manipulation of games robbed the Roman calcio of his innocence. Some sources of financing have dried up, and the clubs have their work cut out to tame their hooligan fans and improve the safety of stadiums. Rome is fortunate to have the Stadio Olimpico, which is considered safe, and has two teams in Serie A, the top league: AS Roma and Lazio Roma. True tifosi have no choice in the question of which club they support: it is predetermined in their genes. A supporter of Lazio who dons a sky-blue scarf to go to the match on Sunday could hardly marry a woman from a red-and-yellow-clad clan that supports AS Roma. If you want to experience true Roman *calcio*, don't get a ticket for the *curva nord*, the end that's occupied by the Lazio fans, or for the south end where the *romanisti* wave their banners. For dates and information, see *www.sslazio.it, www.asroma.it | no guided tours through the stadium*

Pope Francis enjoys meeting believers in person – to the pleasure of the media

Pope Francis canonized his two predecessors John Paul II and John XXIII to sainthood in the presence of Benedict XVI. As the first Jesuit and South American to take the Chair of St Peter, it will remain to be seen whether he holds conservative views on contemporary issues such as the pill, divorce, celibacy and whether he can bridge the deep divide between the Holy See and modern-day Christians. However in 2014, he presided over a public wedding ceremony for 20 couples some of whom were parents of illegitimate children. What's for sure, this new wind blowing in from the Argentinean Pampas is definitely causing a fresh, new approach in the Vatican. To celebrate his birthday on December 17, thousands of believers danced the tango on St Peter's Square in honour of Pope Francis.

SPAGHETTI ABOVE THE SPANISH STEPS

Advertising posters for pasta above the Spanish Steps or billboards for mobile phones and hot rod racing cars pictured on the tarpaulins of scaffolding propping up the crumbling Palazzi: Romans and tourists feel oppressed by the explosion of sponsorship advertising on city monuments. But cultural sponsoring is on trend, as the City of Rome is so short of cash that it could hardly pay for another delivery of bricks for the Colosseum. The fashion house Fendi, which recently donated 1.7 million euros for the restoration of the Fontana di Trevi, no longer commissions large-scale advertising. Instead, the fashion empire staged its latest couture show at the venue: Fendi models ran about like modern-day nymphs on a glass catwalk high above the sparkling fountain. Fortunately, there are also discreet sponsors without much fanfare: the luxury jeweller Bulgari gave 1.5 million euros to clean the Spanish Steps of leftover pizza, chewing gum and red wine. Tod's designer shoe emporium donated 25 million euros for the restoration of the crumbling Colosseum – and no brand advertising. The Roman legionnaires, who pose in front of the structure for tourist photos, walk around in their own plastic sandals, not Tod's designer boots.

SIGHTSEEING

WHERE TO START?
Largo di Torre Argentina (145 D4) (*F9*) is a good starting point for a first exploration of the *centro storico*. From here it is no more than six minutes to Piazza Navona or eight minutes to Campo de' Fiori and your first cappuccino break of the day. To the east it takes only 15 minutes to walk to the Capitoline Hill or half an hour to the Foro Romano and Colosseo. Many buses stop at Largo di Torre Argentina, e.g. no. 40, 60, 62, 63, 70, 81, 95, tram 8. Next parking: Villa Borghese/Viale del Muro Torto (about 5 km/3 mi away)

Are these Romans crazy? Follow the lead of Asterix and Obelix in the famous comic book, "Asterix Conquers Rome". Don't be awestruck by the immense achievements of the ancient civilization or glory of the Baroque period, but conquer the Eternal City in the same relaxed way as both the comic-strip heroes. It's a good idea to take a break and treat yourself to the amazing ice cream or drink a cappuccino. Simply ticking off the highlights can be quite exhausting. You can also take heart because even a genius like Goethe was so overwhelmed by the "churches and palaces, ruins and pillars" at the start of his time in Rome that – at least for a while – the poet was left speechless. But he didn't have to contend with the long queues in front of the main tourist sites.

Fountains, palazzi, monuments galore:
Rome is a vast open-air museum
with amazing potential for adventure

Pre-booking online is recommended for major attractions.

Rome is a vast, glorious open-air museum where you can pick out the top attractions like a gourmet buffet. During its 3000 years, the Eternal City has acquired multiple attractions and art treasures. No computer could produce a catalogue of them all even today. Nowhere else offers so many highlights from such different historic periods that often overlap like a layer cake. There are thrilling crossovers of time and space, above- and below ground. During construction work for the futuristic Parco della Musica auditorium, archaeologists discovered the ruins of a 2000-year-old Roman villa that is now ingeniously integrated into the open-air section of the concert hall. In Rome, antique statues already stand below the River Tiber: some of the art treasures of the Musei Capitolinii are exhibited in the former power station, Montemartini, which is an intriguing contrast of marble and machines. Those who prefer a sportier pace can bike along the first

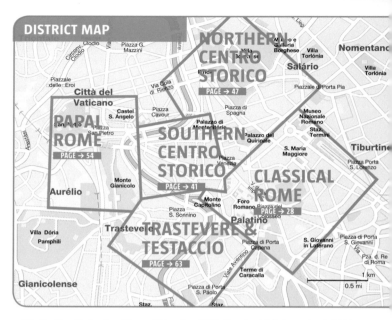

DISTRICT MAP

The map shows the location of the most interesting districts. There is a detailed map of each district on which each of the sights described is numbered.

highway in antiquity, the Via Appia Antica, and in the meantime, walk through the underworld of the Domitilla or Calisto Catacombs. There is something to discover everywhere.

CLASSICAL ROME

From the Capitol to the Lateran: Rome's early age of marble can be found here between the imperial forums, triumphal arches and the Colosseum, as well as one of the finest golden mosaics of the Middle Ages in Santa Prassede.

In Monti, as this popular quarter is called, you can take a trip back in time along

every step of the way: close to the postmodern Stazione Termini you will find the largest baths of ancient Roman times, the majestic Papal basilica Santa Maria Maggiore and Michelangelo's impressive "Moses". Step down into the vaults of the lower church of San Clemente or up to the square at the Capitol. Experience the charm of national traditions around the Piazza Santa Maria in Monti, the nightlife in the Via dei Serpenti or enjoy the Sunday street festival between the Colosseum and the Capitol, when the Via dei Fori Imperiali is closed for traffic.

▪️ BOCCA DELLA VERITÀ ●
(151 E3) (*∅ E10*)

The "mouth of truth" is a strange marble face as tall as a man on the left of the atrium of Santa Maria in *Cosmedin*. The left eye seems to be shedding tears, and only the mouth has been worn smooth, as visitors place their hands into the monster's jaws. By tradition jealous married people send their partners there. If they don't tell the truth, this ancient lie detector is said to bite off the hand. When you take out your hand again with a laugh, briefly visit the 1000-year-old gold mosaic inside the church that was created by the famous artist family of the Cosmaten *(cosmedin*, Greek for ornament*). Daily 9.30am–6pm, in winter 9.30am–5pm | Piazza Bocca della Verità 18 | bus 63, 30, 160, 170, 628*

▓2 CAMPIDOGLIO ★
(145 E–F 5–6) (*Ⓜ F9*)

It's just a magical place, even if nowadays the Romans mainly have practical reasons to climb the wide steps to the Capitol, the ancient seat of the Gods.

Frustrated and grumbling citizens go to the town hall in the Palazzo dei Senatori (straight ahead) to complain to the young mayor, Virginia Raggi, about the inefficient administration or constant strikes of the refuse collectors. As a bridal couple, however, they carry on with a beaming smile to the world's most beautiful Registry Office in the Palazzo dei Conservatori (right). Where the Temples of Jupiter and Juno once stood, in 1536 Michelangelo laid out the trapezium-shaped square of the Capitol, flanked by the *Palazzo dei Senatori*, the *Palazzo dei Conservatori* and the *Palazzo Nuovo*. The pedestal from which the riding Emperor Marcus Aurelius greets passers-by with a raised hand today bears a copy of the original statue dating from the 2nd century, which needed protection from pollution and was moved inside the *Musei Capitolini*. ● ☽ If you take the steps to the left of the Piazza del

---

MARCO POLO HIGHLIGHTS

Campidoglio, you have a wonderful view of the Foro Romano. On the way, pause to look at the small bronze statue of the Roman she-wolf, which Romulus and Remus, the founders of Rome, was said to have raised. If the wolf has a fearsome reputation in other parts of the world, the Romans affectionately regard their fur-clad symbol, which is also the football mascot of AS Roma and a popular tattoo on their toned upper arms. *Piazza del Campidoglio | bus 30, 60, 62, 63, 64, 70, 81, 87, 117, 119, 160*

▨ CIRCO MASSIMO
(151 F3) *(𝄞 F10–11)*

Chariot races were like the Formula 1 of antiquity. The glamour of the Circus Maximus resembled the Grand Priz of Monte Carlo. The Roman Emperor cheered on the death-defying chariot drivers who basked in the glory of fame and riches like today's racing drives Hamilton, Alonso and others. Some Empresses – like the sex-obsessed Messalina – are rumoured to have invited the muscly victors to their bedchamber. The four horse-drawn chariots raced seven times anti-clockwise around the 350-m/1148-ft central barrier. A major crash was likely, the side barriers were unpadded, so injuries were often fatal for horses or their drivers. Horse races were already held here during the Etruscan period in the 7th century BC; Caesar commissioned expansion of the biggest racecourse *(maximus* = largest*)* with marble step seating for about 175,000 spectators; his successors created space for 250,000 racing fans. *"Bread and circuses" (panem et circenses)* were then popular events for seeking pleasure. There were plenty of betting booths where ordinary Romans could gamble their sesterce, as well as the smoke-filled bars and many brothels. Today, the Circus Maximus is a green, peaceful and tranquil place beneath the Palatine. In summer, open-air concerts rekindle a magnificent atmosphere for many tens of thousands of fans. *Via del Circo Massimo | Metro B Circo Massimo | Bus 75 | tram 3*

▨ COLOSSEO (COLOSSEUM) ★
(152 A2) *(𝄞 G10)*

Stamping, the sound of drums and trumpets! Plus, ear-splitting shouts from the ranks when a gladiator falls to the ground wheezing. Metal glinted in the sunlight, while the dust was stirred up. The Emperor fanned air towards him with a handkerchief; with the same white fragment of fabric that he used to preside over life and death. He usually generously left the decision to his people: the Senators and salaried workers, the nobility

FIT IN THE CITY

There is a lovely jogging route in the park of Villa Borghese: try running from the Galleria Borghese to the Pincio hill, from there to the church of Trinità dei Monti and back via Via Vittorio Veneto – or past the Galleria Nazionale d'Arte Moderna to the Etruscan museum in Villa Giulia, a distance of around three classically beautiful miles.

You can also explore the Centro Storico at a brisk pace by booking a personal trainer for a spot of *Sight Jogging (84 euros per hour | tel. 0 34 73 35 31 85 | www.sightjogging.it)*. The fit, multi-lingual city guides will jog with you along ten cultural routes through the city, even for early-bird tours at 6 or 7 in the morning, when the traffic is still tolerable.

and slaves had the power to send the inferior gladiator to his death with the cry "iugula" ("kill him!"), or occasionally to show mercy and hiss "missum" ("release" or "send away"). Gladiators were professional fighters and highly trained men, yet their social rank was lower than slaves. The winner received a laurel wreath, money and gifts, like the affec-

tivity lasting just eight years. Nowadays, major projects such as airports require a similar timescale just for the planning phase. Technically, the majestic colosseum was also a masterpiece. The arena had seating capacity of 50,000 spectators; the first three rows were reserved for the Roman aristocracy. Women, slaves and plebeians crowded into the top wooden

Where the gladiators once fought: the Colosseum, the largest building in Antiquity

tion of a beautiful lady, and the certainty of getting killed in the next contests.

The gigantic arcades of the Colosseum were Emperor Vespasian's attempt, as successor to cruel Nero, to enhance his popularity with his citizens and staged "bread and circuses", like modern statesmen host the World Cup championships or the Olympic Games. What Vespasian senior had begun in 72 AD was inaugurated by his son and successor, Titus, following an intensive period of building ac-

stand below sun canopies. Today, sophisticated underground passages, trap doors, enclosures and the lifts for wild animals are still exposed in the foundations of the building as well as changing rooms and weapons stores for the gladiators. Safety guidelines were also extremely elaborate: in case of emergency, like a fire, the arena could be cleared in five minutes via 80 entrances and exits.

Today, the Colosseum is not only one of Rome's major attractions with more than five million visitors, but also a proud memorial in opposition to the death penalty. Since 1999 the monument has been bathed in green light every time a state decides to abolish the death penalty. Highly recommended INSIDER TIP are the night tours "La Luna sul Colosseo". *Admission daily 8.30am until one hour before dusk | Admission 12 euros (also valid 2 days for Foro Romano and Palatine), Online reservation recommended at www.coopculture. it | Piazza del Colosseo 1 | Metro B Colosseo*

⑤ FORI IMPERIALI (IMPERIAL FORA)

The Imperial Fora are most beautiful at night when the marble columns are illu-

Reliefs of the Trajan's Column: the emperor's story winds its way to the top

minated and the deeds and main places of action of Caesar or Augustus are brought to life again. Due to the resounding success, the histories and light shows of *"Viaggio nei Fori"* are repeated *(April–Oct daily from 8pm | with headsets available for English or Italian | Info tel. 06 06 08 | www.viaggioneifori.it)*.

Foro di Augusto (151 F1) *(ᗯ F9) (Piazzetta del Grillo 1 | bus 85, 87):* What a detective story from ancient Rome! *The boy* Octavian, whose bronze bust looks slightly anxious, enjoyed a phenomenal rise to fame. After the murder of his great uncle Julius Caesar in 44 BC, the 19-year-old successor prevailed against friend and foe and destroyed Caesar's assassins Brutus and Cassius. He was co-ruler for 13 years, later – as Emperor Augustus – he was the sole ruler for 43 years. He also waged war, but he earns the title of emperor of peace, like Queen Elizabeth II today, due to his stability and continuity. The Forum of Augustus is dominated by the temple of the vengeful Roman god of war, Mars. Augustus had over 80 temples built or adorned. He is said to have found Rome built of brick and left it built of marble. There is a good view from ⬙ Via dei Fori Imperiali.

Foro di Cesare (145 F5) *(ᗯ F9) (Via dei Fori Imperiali | bus 85, 87):* A leader like Donald Trump needs no presidential salary, while Julius Caesar needed no minions of state or subsidies. He had the entire government quarter built at his own expense. Still recognisable are the rows of shops, the remains of the Basilica Argentaria, which was used as a bank and exchange, and three surviving columns of the Temple of Venus. One day, as the historian Suetonius relates, the consul received the senate seated on the base of the Temple of Venus. With this affront to piety – only gods were allowed to sit – Caesar claimed a status

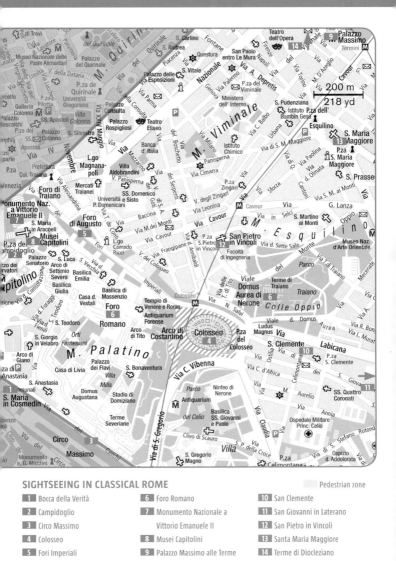

SIGHTSEEING IN CLASSICAL ROME

▨▨▨ Pedestrian zone

1 Bocca della Verità

2 Campidoglio

3 Circo Massimo

4 Colosseo

5 Fori Imperiali

6 Foro Romano

7 Monumento Nazionale a Vittorio Emanuele II

8 Musei Capitolini

9 Palazzo Massimo alle Terme

10 San Clemente

11 San Giovanni in Laterano

12 San Pietro in Vincoli

13 Santa Maria Maggiore

14 Terme di Diocleziano

equal to Jupiter. Shortly afterwards he was murdered.

Foro di Traiano (151 F1) (𝄞 F9) (Tue–Sun 9am until one hour before dusk | Admission 11.50 euros, good view also from out- side | Via IV Novembre 94 | bus 40, 64, 70, 170): One column is exactly like the next, but this one is like a newspaper on a production line. The 38-m/124.7-ft high Trajan's Column, erected in 113 AD,

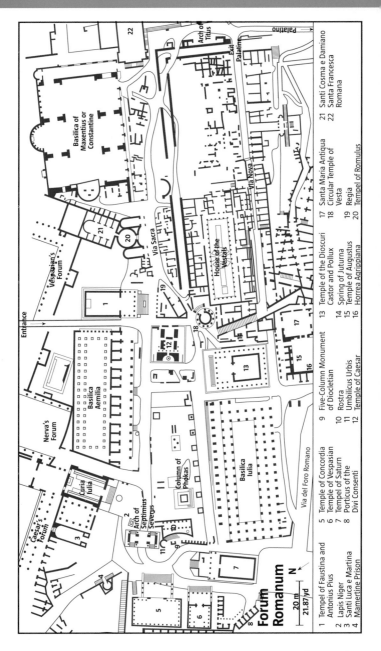

Forum Romanum

N

20 m
21.87/yd

1 Tempel of Faustina and Antonius Pius
2 Lapis Niger
3 Santi Luca e Martina
4 Mamertine Prison

5 Temple of Concordia
6 Temple of Vespasian
7 Tempel of Saturn
8 Porticus of the Divi Consenti

9 Five-Column Monument of Diocletian
10 Rostra
11 Umbilicus Urbis
12 Temple of Caesar

13 Temple of the Dioscuri Castor and Pollux
14 Spring of Juturna
15 Temple of Augustus
16 Horrea Agrippiana

17 Santa Maria Antiqua
18 Circular Temple of Vesta
19 Regia
20 Tempel of Romulus

21 Santi Cosma e Damiano
22 Santa Francesca Romana

In the footsteps of Caesar and Cicero: Forum Romanum, Ancient Rome's political powerhouse

the centrepiece of the last and most magnificent of the imperial forums, now gleams pearly white again after almost ten years of restoration. You can admire the 200-metre/656-ft sculptural frieze depicting Emperor Trajan's war against the Dacians from below.

6 FORO ROMANO ★
(145 F5–6) (*M F9–10*)

From his office in Palazzo Senatorio in the Capitol, the mayor of Rome has the best view of the marble-clad centre of power in the ancient world. The Forum Romanum, originally conceived as a sanctuary of Vesta, evolved from a cattle market to a political arena from which not only Rome but the whole Roman Empire was ruled. This is where Cicero made his flaming orations against Catilina and old Cato spoke his *ceterum censeo*: "Carthage must be destroyed." Today you don't have to wear a toga to stroll between columns and triumphal arches on

warm evenings: INSIDER TIP "Roma sotto le stelle" (Rome beneath the stars) is the name for night tours *(in Italian and English | June–mid-Sept | dates from the tourist information pavilions and newspapers, e.g. La Repubblica)*.

Here are some highlights: From the entrance on Via dei Fori Imperiali you pass the Basilica Aemilia, *Tempio di Faustina, Tempio di Caesare and Arco di Augusto* and cross the Via Sacra to reach the Rostra, the platform for speakers; on the right are the *Lapis Niger,* the Black Stone above the grave of Romulus, the *Curia* of the senate and the *Arco di Settimo Severo;* on the left the *Tempio di Saturno* and *Basilica Julia*, the court building that Caesar had built shortly before he was killed, the rectangular *Tempio di Castore e Polluce* and the *circular. Tempio di Vesta*, where the Vestals, maidens from the highest-ranking families, tended the sacred flame. Along the Via Sacra you pass the *House of the Vestals*, the *Tempio di Romolo*, which Maxentius built for a son who died young, and the *Basilica di Massenzio*, altered by Constantine.

At the entrance near the *Arco di Tito*, a path leads up to Palatine Hill, where many rich Romans, among them Cicero and Catullus, possessed villas. You can walk back down to the forum through lovely 16th-century gardens, the Orti Farnesiani. *Daily 8.30am till one hour before dusk | entrances: Largo Salara Vecchia (Via dei Fori Imperiali), Via di San Grego-rio 30, Piazza Santa Maria Nova (Arco di Tito) | admission 12 euros (includes Colosseo and Palatine, valid 2 days) | pre-booking Tel. 06 39 96 77 00 | bus 85, 87, 117*

■ MONUMENTO NAZIONALE A VITTORIO EMANUELE II
(145 E–F5) (*Ø F9*)

Romans disrespectfully dubbed it "typewriter", "wedding cake" or even "false teeth". A striking construction on Piazza Venezia is a snow-white marble pile, the National Monument in honour of Victor Emmanuel II, the first king of Italy after the achievement of unification in 1870. Now the monument houses the museum of Italian Unification and access to the terrace is from inside. From the ☆ *Terrazza delle Quadrighe*, the highest platform with its decorative bronze horses you get INSIDER TIP a superb view of the Forum Romanum and the whole city centre. *Daily 9.30am–5.30pm, in winter 9.30am–4.30pm | lift 7 euros | Piazza Venezia | entrance from S. Maria in Coeli | bus 30, 40, 85, 87, 119*

■ MUSEI CAPITOLINI ★
(145 E–F 5–6) (*Ø F9*)

How about a change from the Vatican Museums? The Capitoline Museums are smaller, easier to navigate and less overcrowded than the Papal competition. Ironically, they were sponsored by Pope Sixtus IV, who also commissioned the Sistine Chapel. His Holiness wanted to remove the naked statues in the Vatican and left them as a legacy to the city in 1471 – the world premiere of the first public museum. Don't miss five top attractions: the upraised index finger made of marble of the Colossus of Constantine, which presents not exactly the ancient version of giving someone the finger, but is a symbol of power. The "Capitoline Wolf" is housed in

LOW BUDGET

In the state museums, young EU citizens below the age of 18 enjoy free admission; under 25 they get a considerable discount. Don't forget to take ID!

● Every first Sunday of the month, admission to all state (!) museums and archaeological sites such as *Foro Romano* or *Colosseo* is free; at the ● *Vatican Museums* every last Sunday *(9am–12.30pm)* – when they are even more crowded than usual.

The *Biglietto 4 Musei* is valid for three days in the four archaeological museums *Palazzo Altemps, Palazzo Massimo alle Terme, Terme di Diocleziano* and *Crypta Balbi (7 euros)*. The *Archeologia Card* for 27.50 euros is also valid for the *Colosseo, Palatine* and two ruined sites on the *Via Appia Antica*.

With the ATAC day ticket *(biglietto giornaliero)* for 6 euros you can travel all day by bus and Metro throughout Rome. Not valid for the airport train.

The original Emperor Marcus Aurelius on horseback in the Musei Capitolini, its copy stands on the piazza

the Sala della Lupa. It is Rome's symbol and the mother of all Romans, as she suckled Romulus and Remus, Rome's founders with her milk. The delicate Roman "Mosaic of the Doves" where the birds of peace drink from a golden cup, was discovered in Villa Hadrian in Tivoli (Sala delle Colombe). If you want to see a well-built man with rippling muscles, then visit the "The Dying Gaul". The warrior uses his last strength to sit upright – and this is one of the most moving sculptures. Now to return to women and the Goddess of Love: the "Capitoline Venus", shown coming out of her bath naked, was not thought suitable for the Iranian President Rouhani to view during his Rome visit. The statue was covered up with a bathing towel, probably because the Hellenic marble copy is simply stunningly beautiful.

The most spectacular exhibit is the **INSIDER TIP** original equestrian statue of Emperor Marcus Aurelius. Since 2005 it has been placed under a glass roof in the *Giardino Romano*, a courtyard of the Palazzo dei Conservatori. A copy stands on the Capitol square. Treat yourself to a break in the ☕ cafeteria of the roof garden (open to those not visiting the museum) for a breathtaking view of the city! *Daily 9.30am–7.30pm | admission 11.50 euros, with Centrale Montemartini 12.50 euros, with exhibition 15 euros (valid 7 days) | Piazza del Campidoglio | bus 63, 95, 119, 160, 170, 638 | tram 8*

9 PALAZZO MASSIMO ALLE TERME
(148 C5) (*ØⱮ H8*)

Thousands of commuters and passers-by, buses and taxis travel past the Palazzo Massimo at Termini railway station every day. What are they are missing? The museum of antiquities displays the luxurious lifestyle of the rich and beautiful people at that time, just like in a lifestyle magazine. Rome's upper classes commissioned erotic frescoes to decorate the walls of their country villas, and erected majestic statues like the

More beautiful than reality: the Painted Garden, completed over 2000 years ago for the Villa di Livia

"Discus Thrower of Myron" or – totally transgender – the copy of the "Sleeping Hermaphrodite" in the villa gardens. But the museum's highlight is the **INSIDERTIP** ▶ Painted Garden of the Villa of Livia, Rome's first Empress, displayed on the third floor. It's difficult to believe that the delicate frescoes are 2000 years old, and their original colours seem to have been magically placed here. The wall frescoes depict a fantasy dream landscape in which everything is flowering and bursting into leaf at once, regardless of the season. In this former dining hall, the Imperial couple, Livia and Augustus, dined in their villa whenever they had had enough of Rome's exhausting political life. *Tue–Sun 9am–7.45pm | admission 7 euros (also for Palazzo Altemps, Terme di Diocleciano and Crypta Balbi, valid 3 days) | Largo di Villa Peretti 1 | Metro A, B Termini*

🔟 SAN CLEMENTE (152 B2) *(🕮 H10)*
In this church, almost like in an elevator, you can enjoy a short journey back through time to Rome's different historical periods, until you reach the *cloaca massima* and hear the trickling water of antique Rome's drainage system. The golden mosaics of the chancel arch and the apse of the medieval upper church are a gem. You then descend to the lower church (4th century), dedicated to Clement, the fourth pope (88–97), where fragments of frescoes depicting the life of the saint can still be made out. This columned basilica, which the Normans destroyed, lies in turn above a building used for the cult of the Persian god of light Mithras, whom many Roman legionaries worshipped in bloody rituals associated with bulls.
One level below that are the remains of a townhouse from Caesar's period, and

below flows water in the *cloaca massima,* by means of which the Etruscans dried out a swamp nearly 3000 years ago – the prerequisite for building the Forum Romanum. *Mon–Sat 9am–12.30pm, 3–6pm, Sun 12.15pm–6pm | admission 10 euros | Via Labicana 95 | Metro B Colosseo | tram 3*

⑪ SAN GIOVANNI IN LATERANO
(152 C3) (*ω J10–11*)

Quiz question: what is the most important church for Christianity? St Peter's? Wrong! It is the St John Lateran basilica, which was consecrated in 313 AD, and a gift of Emperor Constantine for the Pope at the time. This is the "Mother of All Churches in the City and the world", as the inscription states on the façade. It was the seat of the pontificate for almost 1000 years until he went into exile in the 14th century in Avignon, Southern France. The vast basilica, which always appears slightly sparse and empty, was modified during the Baroque period. The cloister, a place of quiet retreat, and the baptistry are worth seeing.

During the Holy Year 2016, many pilgrims came to the Lateran basilica, and many were attracted to the *Scala Santa,* the Holy Steps, opposite. In memory of the suffering of Jesus, the praying pilgrims move, rather painfully, on their knees up the 28 steps to the Sancta Sanctorum, the chapel for the popes. The steps were allegedly from the house of Pontius Pilate who had Jesus condemned to death on the cross. *Daily 7am–6.30pm, baptistery 7am–12.30pm | Piazza di San Giovanni in Laterano | Metro A S. Giovanni | bus 85, 87 | tram 3*

⑫ SAN PIETRO IN VINCOLI
(152 A1) (*ω G9*)

The church is attractive, but many visitors only arrive to see Michelangelo's powerful and magisterial figure of "Moses" (1516) on the tomb of Pope Julius II. The extremely dynamic marble sculpture has not only fascinated generations of art fans, but even psychologists like Sigmund Freud. Evidently, Moses, shaking with anger, had discovered his followers dancing around the Golden Calf. Moses is still seated there, his hand fondling his long beard, yet he is about to stand with a display of his wrath, when the stone tablets bearing the Commandments seem to slide from under his arm. Moses draws back to keep hold of the tablets. Michelangelo's genius has captured this physical gesture in marble. The name of the church is derived from the chains *(vincoli* = chains*)* with which St Peter is said to have been incarcerated in the Mamertine

Most of the popes were ordained in San Giovanni in Laterano

prison below the Capitol. They are kept as a precious relic below the high altar. *Daily 8am–12.30pm, 3pm–6pm | Piazza di San Pietro in Vincoli 4a | Metro B Cavour*

🔟 SANTA MARIA MAGGIORE
(148 C6) (*ഥ H8*)

Who says it never snows in Rome? Every year on the eve of 5 August in front of Santa Maria Maggiore flowers, scraps of paper or laser beams are used to create a white illusion to commemorate the founding of the church. On this evening in the year 352 the Virgin Mary is said to have instructed Pope Liberius to build a church on the Esquiline Hill where the next morning he would find snow. This is a genuinely impressive church, and incidentally it was the first basilica that Pope Francis visited in 2013 after his election. The patriarchal basilica is not only the largest *(maggiore* = larger) of the 80 churches in Rome dedicated to the Virgin Mary. Its campanile is the city's tallest. Behind the lively Rococo façade are several treasures: the gleaming golden mosaics in the nave and on the chancel arch as well as the stone mosaic floors are among the finest in Rome. One thing emerges to spoil all this: the coffered ceiling from the time of the Borgia popes was covered in the first gold that the Spanish conquerors robbed from the inhabitants of the newly discovered American continent. *Daily 7am–7pm| Piazza Santa Maria Maggiore | bus 70, 71, 75*

🔢 TERME DI DIOCLEZIANO
(148 C5) (*ഥ H7*)

Wellness in the ancient Rome! Opposite Stazione Termini lie the largest Roman baths, which today are part of the collection of antiquities of the *Museo Nazionale Romano*. Emperor Diocletian inaugurated this temple to hygiene and relaxation in 306 AD with huge water

Campo de' Fiori: Rome's favourite square for market shopping and a meal in romantic surroundings

basins and baths for 2400 visitors. In the Baroque period a Carthusian monastery designed by Michelangelo and the church of *Santa Maria degli Angeli* were constructed over the ruins of the bath. In the *Chiostro di Michelangelo* thousands of inscriptions convey an idea of life in ancient times. *Daily 9am–7.45pm | admission 7 euros (also valid for Palazzo Altemps, Palazzo Massimo and Crypta Balbi) | entrance Via Enrico de Nicola 79 (near Stazione Termini) | Metro A, B Termini, Piazza dei Cinquecento*

SOUTHERN CENTRO STORICO

The heart of the historic city, the "Centro Storico" with its Renaissance and Baroque palaces, gushing fountains and crooked alleys, lies between Via del Corso, Piazza Venezia and the bend in the Tiber.

This is also the political epicentre of Italy. Piazza Colonna, where the Column of Marcus Aurelius tells of victories in battle against the Marcomanni, is the site of Palazzo Chigi, the seat of the prime minister. Behind it on Piazza Montecitorio is the national parliament, whose members recently have not always been known for accomplishing glorious deeds. Since 1946 the country has elected 66 Prime Ministers. A walk through the narrow streets will almost automatically bring you to Piazza Navona, a Baroque arena for people-watching, and to Campo de' Fiori. In recent times not everything has been rosy in the heart of Rome. Exorbitant rents have driven out many of the old residents, and the ironsmiths and basket weavers can't keep their heads

above water in the rising tide of fashion boutiques.

■ CAMPO DE' FIORI ★ ●
(144 C5) (*m D9*)

Here is a lively party atmosphere. This is the piazza for meeting in the evening and is especially popular with young people. At the centre of Rome's popular square, surrounded by tall and restored palazzi, stands a memorial to the Dominican monk, Giordano Bruno, who was burned at the stake here by the Inquisition at the start of the Holy Year of 1600. From beneath his hood Bruno looks defiantly towards the Vatican past the lively goings-on of the market in the mornings and the party people and restaurant-goers in the evenings. On Rome's favourite vegetable market fewer stands are to be found nowadays than in the past, as the competition from supermarkets takes its toll, but many Roman women still swear by the Campo, where lots of greens, root vegetables, spices and even clothes are on sale, though not many flowers despite the name of the square, which comes from a flower-covered meadow that was here in the Middle Ages. *Bus 40, 62, 63, 64*

■ GALLERIA DORIA PAMPHILJ
(145 E4) (*m E8*)

If you want to know how decadently Rome's aristocracy lived and lavished their wealth, then the Palazzo Doria Pamphilj is a perfect example. The Rococo façade of the Palazzo on Via del Corso has recently been renovated. Behind it, in a gallery decorated with gold and frescoes, on walls of silk wallpaper, artworks by Titian and Velazquez hang in rows, sometimes three paintings one above the other – and also the famous portrait of the Pamphilj Pope Innocent X, who was anything but a devout and benign father of the church. *Daily 9am–7pm | admission 12 euros | Via del Corso 305 | www.doriapamphilj.it | bus 62, 63, 117, 119*

▣ GALLERIA SPADA (144 C5) *(𝄞 D9)*

The palazzo of 1540 is itself a masterpiece of playful Italian architecture. Join in the confusion created in the courtyard by the INSIDERTIP play on perspective that Francesco Borromini designed for Cardinal Bernardino Spada. The statue

Ferro 13 | www.galleriaspada.benicultur ali.it | bus 62, 64

▣ GHETTO/MUSEO EBRAICO (145 D6) *(𝄞 E9)*

The Jewish ghetto lies in the heart of Rome and has seen good and bad times. Today, it is a popular and lively quarter where Jewish tradition and kosher cuisine thrive again. The first Jews settled here as early as the 2nd century BC, which puts them among the true *roma-*

Rabbi in the Old Synagogue, today open to the public as the Museo Ebraico

of Mars seems to be large and some distance away from you, but the passageway is in reality only 9 m/29.5 ft long and the statue 1 m/3.3 ft high. The optical illusion was achieved by decreasing the size of the colonnade towards the back. The upper floor is home to an excellent collection of paintings by the stars of the 17th and 18th centuries, such as Annibale Carracci, Titian, Guido Reni, Domenichino and Caravaggio. *Wed–Mon 8.30am–7pm | admission 6 euros | Piazza Capo di*

ni romani, the oldest citizens of Rome. Roman law granted them equality and religious freedom for centuries until the missionary zeal of the Christians made them a persecuted minority. In the Middle Ages and Baroque period they suffered under narrow-minded popes, who made them race against horses along Via del Corso as a popular amusement. In 1555 Pope Paul IV built a wall around the ghetto, and this confinement was not lifted until the time of the republic in 1870.

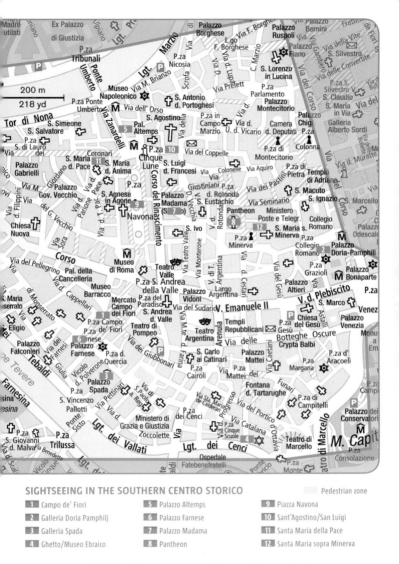

SIGHTSEEING IN THE SOUTHERN CENTRO STORICO

▨▨▨ Pedestrian zone

1 Campo de' Fiori
2 Galleria Doria Pamphilj
3 Galleria Spada
4 Ghetto/Museo Ebraico

5 Palazzo Altemps
6 Palazzo Farnese
7 Palazzo Madama
8 Pantheon

9 Piazza Navona
10 Sant'Agostino/San Luigi
11 Santa Maria della Pace
12 Santa Maria sopra Minerva

The worst day in the ghetto, however, was 16 October 1943, when the Gestapo herded 2091 Jews onto trucks at the Portico d'Ottavia and deported them to death camps. Entire families were wiped out.

Only 16 survivors, and only one woman, returned. Today, Jewish life is flourishing again. Around the popular *Fontana delle Tartarughe,* or Turtle Fountain by Taddeo Landini, where four young adolescents have hands raised to help bronze turtles drink from the basin, there is also a party mood in the evenings. The Roman *Teatro Marcello,* which was begun by Julius Caesar and completed by his successor Augustus, is now an archaeology park, and in summer classical concerts are held here. In the old synagogue the *Museo Ebraico (Sun–Thu 10am–6pm, June–Sept 10am–5pm, Fri 9am–2pm, Oct–May Sun–Thu 9.30am–4.30pm | admission 11 euros | Lungotevere Cenci | www.museoebraico. roma.it)* displays precious silver items and robes, and organises guided tours through the ghetto. *Bus 23, 63*

⑤ PALAZZO ALTEMPS
(144 C2) (*ℳ D8*)

His Excellency simply had good taste – only ever the best. The Austrian Cardinal Hohenems, who was renamed Cardinale Altemps in Rome, acquired a palazzo in 1568 adjacent to Piazza Navona. He furnished the building with the very best that the artworld had to give. The wall frescoes alone and wooden panelled ceilings of the palazzo as well as the loggia in the courtyard are impressive. Not forgetting Aphrodite, Apollo, Hermes and Ares: the marble statues of the gods from the Ludovisi Collection have captivated many visitors. Art can be so cool! *Tue–Sun 9am–7.30pm | admission 7 euros (ticket includes Palazzo Massimo, Crypta Balbi and Terme di Diocleciano, valid for 3 days) | Piazza Sant' Appollinare 46 | bus 70, 81, 492*

⑥ PALAZZO FARNESE
(144 B5) (*ℳ D9*)

The elegant Palazzo Farnese near Campo de' Fiori is occupied by the French embassy. Usually, for security reasons, it is not even possible to sneak a glance inside the courtyard, which Michelangelo designed in 1546. The beautiful gallery with famous frescoes by Annibale Carracci is being restored, but you can join one of the guided tours to see parts of the palace, arranged by the organisation *Inventer Rome (mobile tel. 34 93 68 30 13 | www.inventerrome.com). Piazza Farnese 67 | bus 40, 62, 64*

⑦ PALAZZO MADAMA
(144 C3) (*ℳ D8*)

Pope Clement VII (1523–34) de' Medici pulled off the political feat of marrying off his illegitimate son Alessandro to the illegitimate daughter of Emperor Charles V, Margaret of Parma. "Madama", as she was fondly called by the people of Rome, only lived in this Renaissance palace, where her husband was murdered, for a year. Since 1871 it has been the seat of the Italian senate. *Piazza Madama | bus 70, 81, 87, 492*

Baroque stage with a party atmosphere: Piazza Navona with the Fountain of Neptune

■8 **PANTHEON** ★ (145 D3–4) (*⑪ E8*)

A cylinder with a dome on top: the Pantheon, built in 27 BC at the behest of Marcus Agrippa, the son-in-law of Augustus, to honour all the gods, is a seemingly simple construcion. From the outside, the 2000-year-old temple looks slightly grey and pockmarked, but when you walk through the high, bronze doors you will be surprised: inside, you marvel at the largest, unsupported dome of ancient Rome with a giant, open skylight. On sunny days, the effects of light are astonishing, and even more so if it rains, when water drains through a recess at the centre of the building. Why does this ancient temple – rebuilt by Emperor Hadrian, desecrated in the Middle Ages as a church and requisitioned as a memorial space for the Italian royal family – lie conveniently for tourists at ground level, when in the age of classical Rome, it was entered by ascending five steps? In the course of time the city piled up 6 m/19.7 ft of rubble, and the architecture of antiquity sank beneath it all. *Mon–Sat 8.30am–7.30pm, Sun 9am–6pm | free admission | Piazza della Rotonda | bus 40, 62, 64*

■9 **PIAZZA NAVONA** ★ ●
(144 C3–4) (*⑪ D8*)

You cannot miss it! The most beautiful and cheerful arena of the Baroque period, elongated but enclosed, lively and colourful but at the same time intimate, is the work of Renaissance and Baroque popes, like so many attractive squares and streets in Rome. To please his beloved sister-in-law Olimpia, Innocent X (1644–55) not only ordered the construction of Palazzo Pamphilj, today the seat of the Brazilian embassy, for her, but also spread this wonderful piazza at her feet. It was laid out on the site of the *circo agonale*, out of which the people of Rome made the word *navona*. Until the late 18th century princes of the Church and patrician families enjoyed contests and horse races here from the windows of their palaces. To cool the Romans down in the summer, the piazza was flooded in August so that miniature naval battles could be staged. This Baroque arena is to this day a superb stage for poor performers and wealthy show-offs, mediocre artists and street hawkers, well-known people about town and mongrels who trot to and fro past the ever-busy tables of the cafés.

Gianlorenzo Bernini's *Fontana dei Quattro Fiumi*, is the centre of attention on the piazza. Four river gods are seated on a rocky grotto crowned by an obelisk. They represent the Danube, Nile, Ganges and Rio de la Plata. The last of these has taken up such a defensive posture that he seems to be afraid that the church of Sant'Agnese opposite is about to collapse – and indeed, the church was designed by Bernini's rival Francesco Borromini. This is, however, a myth, as the Baroque church was built two years after completion of the fountain. *Bus 40, 64, 70, 81, 492*

10 SANT'AGOSTINO/SAN LUIGI DEI FRANCESI (144 C2–3) (*ⁿⁿ D8*)

Sant'Agostino is a church of women. Expectant mothers always prayed for a smooth birth to the classically beautiful statue of "La Madonna del Parto" (*parto* = childbirth*)* with her healthy infant Jesus. This was once vital when many young mothers died during childbirth – and their newborns as well. Even today, many pregnant women say a quick prayer to the Madonna. Otherwise, they also turn to their mothers, or part-

ly their grandmothers still wearing black who linger in silent prayer to the Virgin Mary created by the Florentine sculptor Jacopo Sansovino in 1541. Don't miss the painting "Madonna di Loreto" or "Pilgrim's Madonna" in the first chapel on the left of the altar. This painting was created by the infamous Caravaggio in 1605 in his dramatic chiaroscuro style. Not merely his artwork, but his brief, ingenious life fluctuated between light and dark. *Daily 7.45am–12.30pm, 4pm–7.30pm | Piazza Sant'Agostino | bus 70, 81, 116, 492*

If you want to find out more about this 'bad boy' of the Baroque period, only 300 m/984 ft away you can visit the church of *San Luigi dei Francesi (daily 10am–12.30pm, Fri–Wed also 3pm–7pm | Piazza S. Luigi dei Francesi (behind Palazzo Madama) | Bus 70, 81, 87, 492)*. Usually in a drunken state, the ruffian, Caravaggio, was fleeing from the Vatican police when the French granted him a safe hiding place. He repaid the small church of the French with a tremendous legacy of three of his masterworks. However, the dramatic scenes from the life of Matthew caused a scandal because the disrespectful Caravaggio had created semi-naked portraits showing the saint as rather too human.

11 SANTA MARIA DELLA PACE (144 B–C3) (*ⁿⁿ D8*)

The cloister, art, coffee and light snacks offer a charming mixture here. They are located in the ★ *Caffetteria Chiostro del Bramante (Mon–Fri 10am–8pm, Sat/Sun 10am–9pm)* on the first floor above the Renaissance cloister created by Florentine star artist Donatello Bramante. Before or after you enjoy a cappuccino you can visit one of the numerous touring exhibitions in the cultural centre INSIDER**TIP** *Chiostro del Bramante* *(daily 10am–9pm | Arco della Pace 5).* Wonderful! *Via della Pace 5 | bus 30, 40, 62, 64, 70, 492*

12 SANTA MARIA SOPRA MINERVA (145 D4) (*Ø E8*)

Elephants are not necessarily always giant-size! In front of the church of *Santa*

(1521) holding the cross and the instruments of his martyrdom; the bronze loincloth was welded on at a later date. The Cappella Caraffa in the south transept holds famous frescoes by Filippo Lippi that tell the life story of St Thomas Aquinas (1492). *Daily 8am–7pm | Piazza della Minerva | bus 40, 62, 64*

Rome's most expensive shopping mile: from Via Condotti to Piazza di Spagna

Maria sopra Minerva stands a miniature elephant with an enormous saddlecloth. The sculpture by the Baroque artist Bernini is affectionately known as "Minerva's Chick". The small animal also carries an ancient Egyptian obelisk, over 5 m/16.4 ft high, on his back. As though he were not already carrying enough weight, at night-time hooligans have now also broken one of his tusks – much to the horror of many Romans. The only Gothic church in Rome was built for the Dominican order in 1280 above the ruins of a temple dedicated to Minerva. To the left of the altar is Michelangelo's powerful figure of Christ

NORTHERN CENTRO STORICO

The fashion district between the Spanish Steps and Via del Corso offers Haute Couture shopping. In the old Roman palazzi, the numerous boutiques for *alta moda* seem twice as elegant.

Via del Corso used to be the youthful shopping strip for cheap clothing. Now new luxury boutiques like that of the five Fendi sisters invite you to do some

Richard Meier designed a modern shelter for the ancient Roman Altar of Peace, the Ara Pacis

high-class shopping. The most exclusive streets are Via Condotti and Via del Babuino, and the cheapest is Via del Tritone.

When the retail experience has worn you out, stop by the Fontana di Trevi or pay a call to the president of Italy in the Quirinal Palace. If he is not there to receive you, at least there's a good view from the 🔆 piazza with the Dioscuri.

■1 ARA PACIS AUGUSTAE
(147 E4) (𝄞 E7)

An INSIDER TIP ultra-modern construction of steel and glass surrounds Emperor Augustus' 2000-year-old Altar of Peace: this project by the American architect Richard Meier drew a barrage of criticism much like the reaction to the glass pyramid at the Louvre in Paris. But after ten years of complaints and protests, the people of Rome have come to accept the structure. Across from there is the *Mausoleo di Augusto*, commissioned

by the emperor himself, which was built in 27 BC, while Augustus ruled for a further 41 years. *Tue–Sun 9am–7pm | admission 10.50 euros | Lungotevere in Augusta | bus 70, 81*

■2 INSIDER TIP CASA DI GOETHE
(147 E4) (𝄞 E6)

What does Andy Warhol have to do with Goethe? Goethe's famous portrait in the Roman Campagna and its colourful Pop Art version by Warhol are both displayed in the cultural forum at the Casa di Goethe in Rome. Goethe, a classical poet, was already a connoisseur of Italian culture two hundred years ago. "O, how happy I feel in Rome! To think of the time when a grey northern day was around", said the German poet and all-round genius, who spent 15 months in Rome in 1786–87. The apartment that he shared with his painter friend Heinrich W Tischbein is a museum and cultural venue for twenty years now. *Tue–*

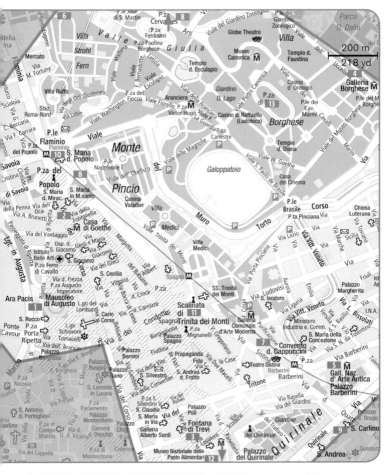

SIGHTSEEING IN THE NORTHERN CENTRO STORICO

///// Pedestrian zone

Sun 10am–6pm | admission 5 euros | Via del Corso 18 | www.casadigoethe.it | bus 117, 119

3 FONTANA DI TREVI (TREVI FOUNTAIN) ★ (145 E–F3) (⌀ F8)

The film scene from "La dolce vita" is legendary. Trevi Fountain owes its world-class reputation to the film. However, on that ice-cold February evening in 1960 when Marcello Mastroianni, who was then Italy's top film star, was supposed to climb into the fountain with Anita Ekberg, life was anything but sweet. The film was almost a flop. The blonde Swede with low-cut décolleté was used to the chilly waters of the Baltic Sea, but her partner Mastroianni, who often played the Latin lover to perfection, emerged as an Italian wimp and went on strike on the edge of the fountain. Only when star director, Federico Fellini, agreed to let him wear hip-high angler's waders beneath his black trousers and dinner jacket was the highly erotic scene a success – and the myth was born of everlasting "dolce vita" in Rome. At that time, the small Piazza, which now attracts a stream of visitors from all over the world both day and night, was deserted apart from Fellini's film team.

It was the last great monument of the Baroque popes, whose power was waning by 1750, the year of its construction. The god of the sea, Oceanus, rides through a triumphal arch with two horses. Incidentally, tourists not only arrive because of "La dolce vita". Those who throw a coin into the fountain will return to Rome at some point in the future. Perhaps it will work. *Piazza di Trevi | bus 62, 63, 81, 85, 95, 492*

▮ GALLERIA BORGHESE ★
(148 B2–3) (⌂ G5)

Miracles happen, but in the Eternal City they sometimes take an eternity: after a 17-year restoration, the Baroque pleasure palace of Cardinal Scipione Borghese reopened. The prelate was one of the world's great patrons of art. Ever since there has been a rush for admission tickets that are only available online. On the ground floor you will see Bernini's sculptures "Daphne and Apollo", "David", "The Rape of Proserpina" and the semi-nude "Paolina Borghese", Napoleon's sister, by Antonio Canova. If you get carried away and want to upload a picture of Bernini's nude sculptures to your best friend or girlfriend on Facebook, please be careful. A "David" with machine gun instead of a stone sling may be acceptable to American online censors, but Mark Zuckerberg's social media network gets serious when it comes to naked breasts and bottoms – as an Italian user discovered when she posted a photo of a naked figure of Neptune in Bologna.

On the first floor, however, you are on the safe side. Here, mainly clothed figures are displayed by the artists Lucas Cranach, Titian, Paul Veronese, Raphael, Peter Paul Rubens and Caravaggio. *Tue–Sun 8.30am–7.30pm | admission 15 plus 2 euros | registration only (Italian/English) tel. 0 63 28 10 or www.ticketeria.it | Piazza Scipione Borghese 5 | www.galleriaborghese.it | bus 52, 53, 490*

Where should all the Etruscan treasures be kept? They found space at the papal Villa Giulia

5 GALLERIA NAZIONALE D'ARTE MODERNA (147 F2) (*M E–F4*)

Modern art has a tough time in a city that is so saturated with historic attractions. Nevertheless, the curators present numerous wonderful 19th/20th century paintings and sculptures, including by Giorgio de Chirico, Gustav Klimt, Vincent van Gogh, Henry Moore, Picasso, Mondrian and Jackson Pollock. The white palazzo was built in 1911 for the International Exhibition of Art in Rome. The rooms are light and the Villa Borghese park is nearby. The well-stocked museum shop has an entertaining product range: *Libreria Gnam. Tue–Sun 8.30am–7.30pm | admission 13 euros | Viale delle Belle Arti 131 | www. gnam.beniculturali.it | tram/bus 3, 19*

6 MUSEO NAZIONALE ETRUSCO DI VILLA GIULIA (147 E2) (*M E4*)

Why is his smile so wide? "Apollo di Veio", the 2500-year-old highlight of the Etruscan museum, looks even more attractive than before his rejuvenation.

However, his most recent facelift hit the headlines, as his restoration was paid for by a tobacco group that wanted to enhance its not so glamorous image with art sponsoring. But the deal gifted the otherwise rather sleepy Etruscan museum sensational admission statistics.

The elegant Villa Giulia, like all Rome's other villas, was a summer residence for the popes, this time Pope Julius III in the 16th century. For more than a hundred years the villa has housed finds from necropolises, the Etruscan grave sites in Latium, Umbria and Tuscany. The most moving exhibit is the "Sarcofago degli Sposi", the tomb of the married couple from the 6th century BC. The ancient couple looks stress-free and radiates more harmony and devotion than many contemporary couples. Did they know that many of the sophisticated grave goods, golden necklaces and rings would be copied and sold today as modern jewellery? *Tue–Sun 8.30am–7.30pm | admission 8 euros | Piazzale di Villa*

Giulia 9 | www.villagiulia.beniculturali.it | tram/bus 3, 19

▓7▓ MUSEO DEI PADRI CAPPUCCINI
(148 A5) (*ᗅ* F7)

On Via Veneto a macabre but space-saving charnel-house admits visitors. Skull piled on skull, bone on bone: this is how Capuchin monks buried some 4000 of their brothers in tombs beneath *Santa Maria della Concezione* in centuries past. *Daily 9am–7pm | admission 8.50 euros | Via Veneto 27 | bus 52, 63*

▓8▓ PINCIO/PIAZZA DEL POPOLO ☼
(147 E–F3) (*ᗅ* E6)

Nothing is more romantic than standing at the INSIDER TIP *Pincio to watch the sun go down behind the roof-tops of Rome.* On the piazza below are the twin churches of *Santa Maria dei Miracoli* and *Santa Maria* in Montesanto that look more interesting from the hill-top than they do from inside. *The Piazza del Popolo* was once a kind of Roman reception area for all pilgrims and travellers entering the Eternal City from the Via Cassia or Via Flaminia. When Queen Christina of Sweden appeared at the gates in 1655, Bernini had just finished altering Michelangelo's gateway so elegantly as it appears today. The Piazza of the People *(popolo = people)* is now a meeting point for demonstrations and protest marches, as the buses filled with demonstrators have easy access outside the Porta del Popolo. In the distance, you can see the green shores of the River Tiber and Michelangelo's dome of San Pietro. *Metro A Spagna, Flaminio*

▓9▓ SAN CARLO/SANT'ANDREA AL QUIRINALE **(148 A–B5) (*ᗅ* G8)**

Beauty contests also exist for churches! In 1638, Bernini's rival Borromini had already started work on a Baroque gem, INSIDER TIP *San Carlo (Mon–Fri 10am–*6pm, Sat 10am–1pm, Sun 12 noon–1pm | Via del Quirinale 23/Via delle Quattro Fontane | bus 40, 64, 70),* with an oval dome on which he worked until his death in 1667. The concave and convex forms of the curved façade with its angel medallion are an architectural masterpiece. Only a few steps away is another highlight, the church of *Sant'Andrea al Quirinale (Tue–Sun 8.30am–12 noon, 2.30pm–6pm | Via del Quirinale 29),* a Baroque late work of Bernini. This is a popular church for weddings with its unusual layout like a salon in old rose, gold and white.

▓10▓ SANTA MARIA DEL POPOLO
(147 E3) (*ᗅ* E6)

Here, the Rome pilgrim Martin Luther celebrated mass with his Augustinian monks in 1510 before he turned away in

anger form the papacy – and proclaimed the Reformation. The beautiful church, which is just behind the Porta del Popolo, was constructed in the 11th century to exorcize Nero's evil spirit that supposedly haunted the place. Inside, visitors are treated to an artistic feast: the frescoes in the choir and Cappella Rovere are by Pinturicchio; in the Cappella Cerasi, to the left of the altar, are the "Conversion of St Paul" and "Crucifixion of St Peter" by Caravaggio, the genius and bad boy of the Baroque period. The Cappella Chigi, the second from the right, was decorated by Raphael for a family of bankers; in the choir are two tombs by Andrea Sansovino; the marble figures of the high altar, on which is the "Madonna del Popolo", are the work of Bernini and Lorenzetto. That's quite a list of famous artists! *Mon-*

Sat 7.30am–12.30pm, 4–7pm, Sun 8am–1.30pm, 4.30–7.15pm | Piazza del Popolo 12 | Metro A Flaminio

🔟 SCALINATA DI TRINITÀ DEI MONTI (SPANISH STEPS) ★ ●
(145 E1) (*🛱 E–F7*)

The Spanish Steps always were the favourite place for Rome travellers – sometimes there are also disadvantages. In the late 18th century the English poets like John Keats and Percy Bysshe Shelley at least sat quietly writing their poetry on the curved balustrades that were built by Alessandro Specchi and Francesco di Sanctis in 1723. Today, the wide steps are filled with young Romans and tourists, even though picnics, drinking, smoking weed and playing guitar are officially banned (and usually ignored in

Possibly the most famous steps in the world: Scalinata di Trinità dei Monti, the Spanish Steps

the Italian way), but flirting is allowed. The popularity of the Spanish Steps has also increased the rubbish that millions of fans discard from fast-food outlets. The jeweller Bulgari, whose luxury store is just behind with a view of the Spanish Steps, recently paid 1.5 million euros for the restoration of the elegant steps. A sticky mass of burgers, pizzas and chewing gum was removed and red wine and ketchup stains were also cleaned. Bulgari also restored the tinkling *Fontana della Barcaccia,* the fountain in the shape of an old boat, and designed in 1629 by Pietro Bernini, the father of the even more famous sculptor Gianlorenzo Bernini, and now flowing crystal clear at the foot of the Spanish Steps. But on Rome's favourite square litter is still quietly left behind. *Metro A Spagna*

🟦12 SCUDERIE DEL QUIRINALE
(148 A6) (*𝄞 F8*)

Where once horses whinnied in the papal stables, you can now view major changing exhibitions. 🔅 **INSIDER TIP** The view from the staircase is fantastic. *Opening times vary | Via XXIV Maggio 16 | www.scuderiequirinale.it | bus 60, 64, 70, 71, 170*

🟦13 VILLA BORGHESE
(148 A–B 2–3) (*𝄞 F5*)

This is the city's majestic recreation park that many Romans associate with happy childhood memories. Here, they played football with their fathers, learned pony riding, slid in a rowing boat across the *laghetto,* the small lake. Today, the park is popular with joggers, cyclists and rickshaws or Segways also glide almost silently through the avenues of cypress trees. You can also simply relax on a bench in the sunshine and listen to the small fountain or the smartphone ringtones of neighbours seated on the bench. You can even go online, as the Villa Borghese offers free WiFi zones. In May, the equestrian tournament is held at the *Piazza di Siena*. At the north end of the park the 🌐 **INSIDER TIP** former zoo is now an ecological park *(April–Oct daily 9.30am–7pm, otherwise 9.30am–5pm | admission 15 euros)* with many native animals, from frogs to a Capitoline Wolf. *Via Pinciana | bus 52, 53, 490, 495 | tram 3, 19*

PAPAL ROME

It is the world's smallest city, but for one billion people it's the centre of their faith. If you would like to get more than a fleeting impression of the Vatican with St Peter's Basilica, St Peter's Square and the Castel Sant'Angelo, allow plenty of time. The Vatican Museums including the Sistine Chapel are not only home to the world's greatest collection of art treasures: in the tourist season they also have the longest queues.

🟦1 CAMPO SANTO TEUTONICO
(146 A–B5) (*𝄞 A8*)

This small oasis is a space of commemoration for the Germans in Rome. The entrance is behind the left-hand colonnade of San Pietro, and if you say the magic words "Campo Santo Teutonico", the Swiss Guard will let you through. The little cemetery in front of the Collegio Teutonico is the last resting place of writers like Stefan Andres, the archaeologist Ludwig Curtius and many German pilgrims who reached Rome and never returned home. *Daily 7am–noon | Via della Sagrestia 17 | bus 40, 64*

🟦2 CASTEL SANT'ANGELO
(CASTLE OF THE HOLY ANGEL) 🔅
(144 A1–2) (*𝄞 C7*)

This fortification, a place of refuge for

the popes, was built above the cylindrical mausoleum of Emperor Hadrian (117–138 AD). It owes its name to a legend dating from Christmas in the year 590, angels in peace. *Tue–Sun 9am–7pm, Fri until 10pm | admission 10 euros | www.castelsantangelo.beniculturali.com | bus 23, 40, 62*

From Castel Sant'Angelo the view ranges far and wide across the roofs of Rome

when at the peak of a plague epidemic the Archangel Michael appeared to Pope Gregory I and sheathed his sword. With this gesture the plague ended. Since 1281 the castle has been connected to the Vatican Palace by a covered passage, the *passetto*. Behind its strong walls are located magnificent apartments for the popes, storerooms and some less-than-angelic torture chambers for heretics too. **INSIDER TIP** In July and August, concerts take place at the roof terrace. From the battlements you get a fantastic view of Rome's most beautiful bridge, the *Ponte Sant'Angelo*. Fortunately it is open only to pedestrians, so you can admire Bernini's ten Baroque

3 GALLERIA NAZIONALE VILLA FARNESINA (144 A5) *(ᗰ C9)*

Parties held in the small palazzo on the River Tiber were famous throughout the city, especially the grand finale. After the banquet the rich banker Agostini Chigi had the dirty cutlery thrown into the Tiber before horrified guests. However, usually bankers are good at calculations: the waiters had beforehand spread invisible nets under water, and as soon as the last guest had left, they fished the expensive silver cutlery from the Tiber again. The small Renaissance building dates from 1508 by the artist Baldassare Peruzzi who also painted the playful perspective frescoes. But the fresco "Amor and Psyche" by the great master Raphael is in another league. The owner of the palazzo is said to have been his model, until Chigi became annoyed about the intimacy and expelled the genius. *Mon–Sat 9am–2pm | admission 6 euros | Via della Lungara 230 | www.villafarnesina.it | bus 23, 280*

4 GIANICOLO 🔅
(150 B–C 1–2) (*Ⅲ B–C 9–10*)

No high-rises spoil the view from the Gianicolo hill – dedicated to the two-faced god Janus – over the domes, churches and palaces of Rome. It is also the site of the equestrian statue of Italian freedom fighter Giuseppe Garibaldi, the hero of the unification of Italy. In 1849 he fought against French troops on this hill. And alongside is Anita Garibaldi, probably the only female rider statue in the world. *Discovery Tour "Trastevere, Gianicolo and the Tiber" (see p. 118). Bus 75, 115, 870*

5 GIARDINI VATICANI (VATICAN GARDENS) (146 A4–5) (*Ⅲ A7*)

The green space of the Vatican: more than half the city-state's area comprises spacious gardens with manicured flower beds, cedars, palms and pine trees. Since the Argentinian Pope Jorge Bergoglio (Pope Francis) has resided here, a colony of green monk parakeets happens also to have settled. The South American parrots, which have probably avoided being kept by a zoo, chatter and screech quite loudly, even when their countryman, the Holy Father, takes his daily walk. Incidentally, Pope Francis doesn't live in the majestic Vatican like his predecessors, but after the conclave he remained in the simple guesthouse at the centre of the garden. The *Necropoli di Santa Rosa*, an ancient Roman burial ground, which was recently discovered beneath the Vatican car park,

are permitted only for tour groups who apply in writing to the *Ufficio Visite Speciali Giardini Vaticani (visiteguidatesingoli.musei@scv.va). Gardens: two-hour guided tours only by prior registration at biglietteriamusei.vatican.va or visiteguidategruppi.musei@scv.va | admission 32 euros, also valid for the Musei Vaticani | tel. 06 69 88 46 76*

6 MUSEI VATICANI (VATICAN MUSEUMS)
(146 B4–5) (*Ⅲ A–B 6–7*)

What do all the visitors want here? Unfortunately, you are not the only visitor of the largest and finest museum in the world! Almost 5 million people make the pilgrimage every year through the thirteen (!) museums to see the ultimate highlight and reward for the crowds – the famous Sistine Chapel.

Four tips on how to view the Vatican Museums: 1) The queues for admission often stretch beyond two or three sections along the Vatican walls. Online advance booking is therefore essential. 2) There are some fans who spend a small fortune, about 2220 euros, to see Michelangelo's frescoes alone. There are also exclusive group tours and official fast-track tickets are available in the morning at 7.30am from 56 euros. Often, polyglot touts approach you in the queue to rip you off with offers like "Sixtine Chapel fast track": be careful, there is no guarantee of quality! 3) What is the best time to visit? Tuesday and Thursday are generally the quietest days, and Wednesday morning is also good when the Pope holds a general audience on St Peter's Square. Avoid Monday when the national museums are closed; then it is twice as full. Those who don't mind crowds and have plenty of patience come on the first Sunday in the month. The crowds are large, but admission is free. 4) The (only) entrance to the

The collections of the Vatican Museums include approximately 50,000 works of art

museums is not inside St Peter's, as many tourists wrongly believe, but at Viale del Vaticano on the north side of the Vatican complex, about ten minutes on foot from St Peter's Square.

Now, it's time to go! The unique art course, which includes 13 museums with about 50,000 objects, is 7 km/4.4 mi long! You shouldn't miss several highlights even if you quickly walk through towards the Sistine Chapel: the *Museo Pio Clementino* displays – archaeologists and art historians are unanimous – the most beautiful and thrilling classical statues in the world. For example, the "Laocoön Group" in the Cortile del Belvedere. The marble group (2nd century BC) shows the Priest Laocoön with his two sons in a dramatic battle with a giant serpent that the Greek Goddess Athena had sent them – as a punishment because the priest wanted to warn the Trojans about the Greeks and their wooden horse. Next, you will see probably the most handsome man in the Vatican, the "Apollo of Belvedere" (Roman copy, 2nd century, of the Greek original, 4th century BC). The antique "Torso of Belvedere" is a parcel of muscles without head, arms and legs, yet the majestic and dynamic rotation of the body is astonishing, and the torso became the preferred model of many Renaissance artists, in particular, Michelangelo. Another beauty is the Roman copy of the "Venus of Knidos" originating from the famous Greek sculptor Praxiteles (4th century BC).

If you follow the tour through the *Pinacoteca Vaticana* you will find the first-class paintings and sculptures from the Middle Ages to the 19th century. This is a VIP show of great artists like Giotto, Fra Angelico, Filippo Lippi, Lucas Cranach, Perugino, Leonardo da Vinci, Titian,

Almost as popular for photos as the exhibited artworks: the staircase of the Musei Vaticani

Veronese, Caravaggio, van Dyck and Bernini. Have we forgotten anyone? You can find the talented painter Pinturicchio represented in the *Appartamento Borgia* where from 1492–95 the artist decorated the rooms of the Borgia Pope Alexander VI with 86 wall and ceiling murals. This was a dark period: here in 1500, the pope's son Cesare Borgia is said to have murdered his brother-in-law, Alfonso d'Aragon, the husband of his sister Lucrezia.

You will find the grand master Raphael displayed in the *Stanze e Logge di Raffaello.* The four halls that Pope Julius II had decorated by him from 1508 are a highlight of Renaissance art. However, the glory of the beautiful completed frescoes didn't last for long. In 1527, during the *Sacco di Roma,* the sack of Rome, the papal apartments were heavily damaged by brutal

Protestant rebels: faces were scratched away and inscriptions were carved like "Luther". The earlier damage to the frescoes was gradually restored. The "School of Athens" fresco, where philosophers Plato, Aristoteles, Pythagoras and Diogenes are in discussion – incidentally, Raphael included a self-portrait along with Michelangelo – as well as the dramatic "Fire in the Borgo" already display freshly restored colours. This is followed by the twelve arcades of the Loggia.

Finally, you arrive where everyone wants to go: in the ★ *Cappella Sistina (Sistine Chapel).* Michelangelo's story of the creation in the papal chapel is resplendent almost in Pop Art colours of lime green, pale purple and orange. The Renaissance genius – also known as *Il Divino,* or "the divine one" – took four years (1508–12) to paint the ceiling frescoes alone with a total

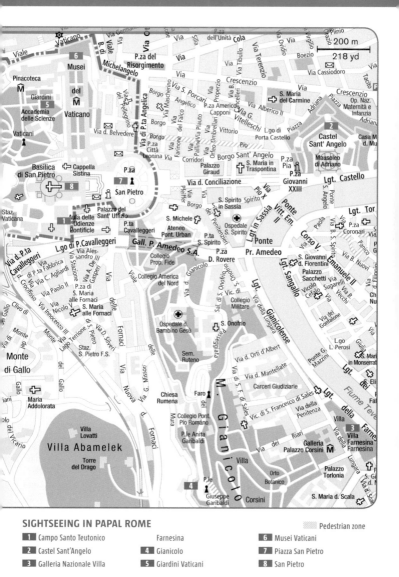

SIGHTSEEING IN PAPAL ROME

▨▨▨ Pedestrian zone

1 Campo Santo Teutonico
2 Castel Sant'Angelo
3 Galleria Nazionale Villa
Farnesina
4 Gianicolo
5 Giardini Vaticani
6 Musei Vaticani
7 Piazza San Pietro
8 San Pietro

length of 41 m/134.5 ft. He worked with his face looking upwards and with a lighted candle on his hat. "My eye is bad, I am not fit to paint", Michelangelo had written to a friend. He would have preferred to create marble sculptures.

What an understatement! He painted a story of the creation with incredible plasticity. The frescoes are unique art-works and relate the creation of light to the story of Adam and Eve and the fall of mankind, the flood and Noah, and set in the context of powerful sibyls and gloomy looking prophets. Of the 340 biblical scenes, the "Creation of Adam", on which the divine spark passes from hand to hand, is the most impressive and certainly the most often reproduced.

More than 20 years later, when Michelangelo was 60 years old, Pope Paul III commissioned him to paint "The Last Judgement" on the end wall of the chapel. When the finished work was unveiled at Christmas 1541, it caused a scandal: a naked Christ was revealed, gathering about him with a regal gesture a whirl of equally naked saints, the chosen, the resurrected and the damned – Michelangelo's superb final flourish.

Rome was on the threshold of the Counter-Reformation, and modern art lovers can count themselves lucky that the pi-

VATICAN CURIOSITIES

Miniature state. Rome's church state is 44 ha/109 acres, not much larger than a medium-size farm – it previously extended across the whole of Central Italy. The 572 residents of the Vatican state have everything, and they don't even pay taxes. The literacy rate is 100 per cent, while population growth is, of course, zero.

What is an ipsophonum? Catholics live around the world – how can Babylonian confusion be prevented? It's easy: Latin is the official Vatican language. The problem is that a lot of contemporary vocabulary is missing in classical Latin. Since 1976 there is a New Latin dictionary in which an answering machine is called an *ipsophonum*, a mobile phone *telephonum manuale* and a cash machine an *automata monetalia*. However, as few members of the congregation actually speak fluent Latin, now Italian, the second official language, is simply preferred.

Railway without trains. The Vatican rail service is the smallest in the world: 400 m/1312 ft tracks, one platform, a single set of points, yet no trains. The Italian railway service provides trains and personnel just in case.

During the last 88 years only four popes have departed from the majestic Vatican railway station. The last was Pope Benedict XVI. However, Benedict usually travelled by helicopter to the papal summer residence Castel Gandolfo. His successor Francis prefers not to take much holiday. He likes to drive himself through Rome in an old Ford Focus.

Popemobile. Pope John Paul II tested the popemobile on an "official visit" in 1979 in his home country of Poland. Afterwards, he introduced it on all of his 104 visits to be as close as possible to the faithful. Most of these 60 papal vehicles remained in the host countries and are re-used for each visit. The current popemobile on St Peter's Square, a converted Mercedes M-Class, only travels at a top speed of 80 km/h/50 mph and weighs five tonnes. The number plate SCV of all Vatican official vehicles stands for **S**tato della **C**ittà del **V**aticano. Or, as the Italians say: **S**e **C**risto lo **v**edesse – if Christ were to see that …

ous counter-reformers did not destroy the work immediately. However, Michelangelo's pupil Daniele de Volterra was obliged to paint some drapery around the loins of the naked figures. When "The Last Judgement" was restored in the 1990s, the restorers washed off 17 of the 40 loincloths. Honour was satisfied for Michelangelo, *Il Divino*, who painted a portrait of himself in the flayed skin of St Bartholomew.

Mon–Sat 9am–6pm (last admission 4pm), last Sun in month 9am–2pm (last admission 12.30pm) | admission 16 euros, last Sun in month free of charge | **INSIDERTIP** *Evening opening (usually with small concerts performed by young virtuoso) May–Oct Fri 7pm–9pm | 16 euros plus 4 euros online charge (book well in advance) | www.museivaticani.va | Chosen time: online booking 4 euros charge (mv.vatican.va | biglietteriamusei.vatican. va); guided tours (www.rome-museum. com, www.througheternity.com) available in English | Metro A Cipro-Musei Vaticani | bus 23, 32, 81*

▣7 PIAZZA SAN PIETRO
(146 B5) (*ळ B7*)

The dome of St Peter's is unique and impressive. St Peter's Square in front of it, completed in 1667, is a masterpiece – and a tour de force of optical illusions. What seems to be a circular space is in fact an ellipse, and the flat-looking rectangle in front of the basilica is a trapezium that rises by 4 m/13.1 ft. Seen from the little marble slabs to the left and right of the fountain, the four rows of columns merge to a single colonnade. The semi-circular colonnades, adorned with statues of 140 saints, are like outstretched, welcoming arms. By such means the Baroque architect Gianlorenzo Bernini achieved his aim of bringing Michelangelo's perfect dome, which al-

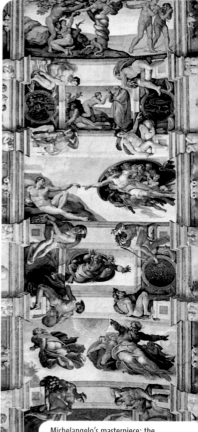

Michelangelo's masterpiece: the ceiling frescoes of the Sistine Chapel

most disappeared behind the ill-proportioned church façade by Carlo Maderno, back onto centre stage. Bernini was aware of this, promising: "You shall only speak of me in terms of great works." *Bus 40, 46, 64, 98*

▣8 SAN PIETRO (ST PETER) ★
(146 B5) (*ळ A–B7*)

St Peter's Basilica can only be described with superlatives. In size it far exceeds

Deacons at the All Saints liturgy in San Pietro, the most important Christian basilica

any other European church, measuring 211 m/692 ft in length (a good 40 m/131 ft longer than St Paul's Cathedral in London), 186 m/610 ft at its widest point and 132 m/433 ft in height. It can hold 60,000 worshippers. In 1506 Pope Julius II gave Donato Bramante the task of building a new church to replace the ancient basilica that Emperor Constantine erected over the tomb of St Peter. In the 120-year period of construction, the best architects in Italy came up with many mutually contradictory models: Bramante wanted a ground plan of a Greek cross (i.e. four equally long arms) with a massive dome, but to meet the wishes of later popes this was changed to a cross with one longer arm. The nave had not been completed when Michelangelo took up Bramante's ideas again in 1546 and started the construction of a large dome on the model of the cathedral in Florence.

Pope Paul V in his turn wanted St Peter's to have the longest nave of any Christian church and awarded Carlo Maderno the commission to extend it and build the façade, which however obstructed the view of the dome.

Inside the church on the right you stand in front of the Porta Santa, the Holy Door, which is opened only in a Holy Year. Michelangelo's "Pietà" is protected by bullet-proof glass in the first chapel on the right, as in 1972 a disturbed young man smashed its nose. On the pillar dedicated to St Longinius, the foot of a bronze statue of St Peter has been polished to a shine by the kisses of pilgrims. Marble steps in front of the papal altar lead down to the tomb of St Peter and the last resting place of Pope John Paul II. Above them stands the bronze baldachin designed by Bernini. The crowds of visitors have made it necessary to move the entrance to the papal tombs and the Vatican catacombs to the right-hand side of the church.

Two further works by Bernini are in the apse: the cathedra altar with the papal throne and the tomb of Urban VIII, a pope from the Barberini family. On the left in the nave is the entrance to the sacristy and the Vatican treasury.

To get up to the roof, where you'll find INSIDER TIP a nice café and souvenir shop, you take a lift to the right of the church (turn right in front of the bronze door). After that 320 steep steps lead up to the ⤵ dome, from where the view of Rome is superb. Be sure to wear decent clothing, i.e. long trousers, no uncovered shoulders! *Church daily 7am–7pm, in winter until 6.30pm, sacristy 9am–6pm, in winter until 5pm | admission 5 euros; roof and dome 8am–6pm, in winter 9am–5pm | admission 5 euros, with lift 7 euros, security checks beneath the right-hand colonnade | Metro A Ottaviano | bus 40, 62, 64*

TRASTEVERE & TESTACCIO

Trastevere, Rome's largest village *trans tiberim* **– i.e. across the Tiber, as it was called in Augustus' day – still has charm, even though recently it has perhaps been prettified and gentrified too much.** Where once washing lines hung across the street and the old folk put their chairs on the pavement in the evening for a chat, an upmarket quarter for clubbing has emerged. Neighbouring *Testaccio* too, once extremely quiet, has a lively nightlife now that bars and clubs have opened in the former slaughterhouse. However, in these districts there are still many residents who would not at any price sell their little apartments full of nooks and crannies. And those who have moved out come back each July for the *Festa de Noiantri.*

■ MONTE TESTACCIO ⤵
(151 D5) *(⑩ D–E 12–13)*

The 120-foot-high Testaccio hill consists of ceramic shards that are thousands of years old – 53 million pieces. This was the site of the wholesale market halls of ancient Rome. As the traders sold their wares in amphorae, instead of merchants' bags, this great historic tip grew up. The old slaughterhouse is now a cultural centre where the contemporary art gallery *MACRO Future (Piazza Orazio Giustinaini 4)* presents special exhibitions. Only guided tour groups can access Monte Testaccio *(registration: tel. 06 06 08). Via Galvani/Via Zabaglia | Metro B Piramide | bus 170, 719, 781*

■ PIAZZA DEI CAVALIERI DI MALTA
(151 E4) *(⑩ E11)*

A spot for romantics and key-hole peepers on the Aventine hill. In 1766 the architect and engraver Giovanni B. Piranesi built the seat of the Order of Knights of St John, which describes itself as a sovereign state and has its own car number plates, though it lacks its own territory. Look through the iron-bound keyhole of the wooden green gate of no. 4, the ● *Buco di Roma* – and you will get a surprising view of St Peter's Basilica in the distance. *Metro B Circo Massimo | bus 30, 60, 75, 118, 175 | tram 3*

■ PIRAMIDE DI CESTIO
(151 E5) *(⑩ E12)*

In ancient times Egypt with its pyramids and obelisks was highly fashionable. That is why the praetor and tribune Caius Cestius had himself buried like a little pharaoh in a luxury pyramid tomb in 11 BC.

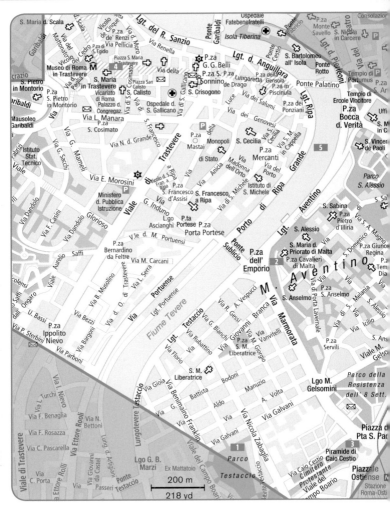

SIGHTSEEING IN TRASTEVERE & TESTACCIO

1 Monte Testaccio
2 Piazza dei Cavalieri di Malta
3 Piramide di Cestio
4 Santa Maria in Trastevere
5 Tevere & Isola Tiberina

The restoration of the ancient obelisk for two million euros was undertaken by the Japanese fashion designer and patron Yuzo Yagi. Incidentally, this was one of the few occasions that something happened ahead of schedule in the Eternal City: the renovation of the Pyramid only lasted 322 days, 75 days fewer than planned. *Piazza Ostiense | Metro B Piramide | tram 3 | bus 23, 60, 83*

4 SANTA MARIA IN TRASTEVERE
(150–151 C–D2) (*ᗞ D10*)

At night-time it is magically illuminated, but in daylight Rome's oldest Church of Our Lady gleams with the 3rd century gold mosaic "Mary and the Ten Holy Women" (12th century). The most beautiful mosaics are in the apse: Jesus larger than life-size with the Virgin and saints. *Daily 7.30am–8pm | Piazza S. Maria in Trastevere | bus H | tram 8*

5 TEVERE & ISOLA TIBERINA
(145 D6) (*ᗞ E10*)

Tevere, or Tiber flows to meet the Mediterranean 20 km/12.4 mi past Rome near Ostia and plays its part in the myth surrounding the founding of Rome as it is believed to be the river into which Romulus and Remus were thrown in a basket as infants. In antiquity INSIDERTIP the island in the river Tiber was dedicated to Aesculapius, the god of healing. Around the year 1000 the church of San Bartolomeo was built on the remains of a temple. The *Ospedale Fatebenefratelli* keeps up the medical tradition to this day. To reach the island, cross the *Ponte Fabrizio* and *Ponte Cestio*, the oldest and most beautiful of the 21 bridges across the Tiber.

Today you can bask in the sun on a man-made beach or enjoy the walking and cycling lanes *piste ciclabili (www.piste-ciclabili.com)* along the promenade. The most attractive section is 10 km/6.2 mi long from Ponte Sublicio to Ponte Milvio.

OUTSIDE THE CENTRE

CENTRALE MONTEMARTINI ★
(155 D4) (*ᗞ E14*)

A radiant white Venus, the Aphrodite of Knidos, Roman emperors, generals and philosophers in a former power station? Don't miss this unusual stage for heroes and gods. *Tue–Sun 9am–7pm | admission 7.50 euros, combined ticket with Musei Capitolini 16 euros | Via Ostiense 106 | Metro B Piramide or Garbatella | bus 716 | tram/bus 3*

Contrasts in the Centrale Montemartini: antique sculptures displayed in a power station

CINECITTÀ (155 D4) (*ᗞ 0*)

Groans, moaning, nerves: do you remember the wild chariot race in "Ben-Hur" with knife blades on the spokes of the warrior chariots, where the drivers risk their own and their horses lives? It's one of cinema's most thrilling scenes! The dream studios are known as Cinecittà – Hollywood on the River Tiber. The 1960s blockbusters were filmed here, as well as the 2010 remake when "Board-

Not much is left any longer of the cinema paradise, but you can tour the backdrop for Scorsese's "Gangs of New York", "Romeo and Juliet" and the Roman buildings of the American sketch comedy series "Rome". *Wed–Mon 9.30am–*

A change of perpective: At MAXXI, the art temple for the 21st century, no angle is like the other

walk Empire" actor Jack Huston steps into the sandals of the old movie star, Charlton Heston. In Cinecittà, cinema spectacles like "Quo Vadis", "Cleopatra" or "Once Upon a Time in the West" also stepped into the international limelight. Cult film director Federico Fellini, who founded Rome's fame as an international film metropolis and party city with "La dolce vita", even had an apartment in the studios.

5.30pm | admission 10 euros, with guided tour 20 euros, 2 euros discount on presentation of Metro ticket | www.cinecitta simostra.it | Metro A Cinecittà

COPPEDÈ QUARTER (148 C–D2) *(Ⓜ H4)*
Not far from Piazza Buenos Aires a gateway opens to a stone-built land of fairytales. This is the strange realm of Gino Coppedè (1886–1924), architect of the "Liberty style", **INSIDER TIP** with Art

Nouveau palazzi and palatial buildings adorned with figures of fairies, spiderlike and fabulous beasts, Babylonian lions' heads and monsters. On *Piazza Mincio* stands a decorative frog fountain surrounded by dainty Villini delle fate, the fairies' houses. *Tram 3, 19 | bus 63*

DIVES IN MISERICORDIA
(155 D4) (*ω 0*)

A must-see for architecture fans: Richard Meier's new steel-and-concrete church in the eastern quarter of *Tor Tre Teste*, approx. 10 km/6.2 mi from the centre. *Daily 7.30am–12.30pm, 4–7.30pm | Largo Terzo Millenio 8–9 | www.diopadremisericordioso.it | Stazione Termini bus 14 to Quarticcolo*

EUR – ESPOSIZIONE UNIVERSALE DI
ROMA (155 D5) (*ω 0*)

For the World Exhibition of 1942, which did not take place on account of the Second World War, Benito Mussolini had this futuristic quarter built halfway between Rome and Ostia. From afar you can see the cuboid *Palazzo della Civiltà del Lavoro* with its 216 window niches. The dome of the *Palazzo dei Congressi* can be counted as an aesthetic example of Fascist architecture, as can the *Museo della Civiltà Romana*, which houses no original works but many excellent copies. The ● *Piscina delle Rose (Viale America 20 | www. piscinadellerose.it)*, Rome's Olympic pool with a length of 50 m, a gym and a spa is also situated here. *Metro B EUR Palasport*

MAXXI ★ ● (155 D4) (*ω C2*)

It will take some while for the shock waves triggered by Zaha Hadid's museum for 21st-century art to die down – for both its admirers and its critics. The *Museo Nazionale delle Arti del XXI. Secolo* near the Stadio Flaminio is an exhibit in itself. Everything is in motion in this building. Ramps suddenly seem to change places as if in a cartoon film, stairs lead up to heaven, and leaning walls or crooked corners tempt visitors to tread new artistic paths at every turn. The collection contains works by such artists as Francesco Clemente, Mario Merz and Gerhard Richter. *Tue–Sun 11am–7pm, Sat until 10pm | admission 12 euros | Via Guido Reni 4a | www.fondazionemaxxi.it | tram 2 | bus 53, 280, 910*

INSIDER TIP▶ PIGNETO
(153 E–F 2–5) (*ω M10*)

The trendy suburb has retained the quirky charm of the 1950s. Jammed in between two arterial roads, Via Prenestina and Via Casilina, this district originally built for railway workers is an area of rented flats, little houses and allotment gardens. Around the main road of the quarter, Via del Pigneto, designers' shops, pubs and literary enoteche have sprung up, as Pigneto has attracted lots of creative people, musicians, gallery owners, designers and young film makers who can no longer afford the high rents in the Centro Storico. The film director Pier Paolo Pasolini found the right milieu of pimps and small-time criminals for "Accattone" in the bar *Necci dal 1924 (Via Fanfulla da Lodi 68)*. No other quarter has so many trendy film clubs, such as *Grauco (Via Perugia 34) and Cineclub Alphaville (Via del Pigneto 283)*. And nature lovers can take a leafy walk beneath a 2000-year-old aqueduct, the *Acqua Claudia. Bus 105 | tram 5, 14*

TERME DI CARACALLA
(152 B4–5) (*ω G12*)

The romantic ruins of the Terme di Caracalla became famous thanks to the first concert for the 1990 World Cup when the three tenors Luciano Pavarotti, José Carreras and Plácido Domingo raised their powerful voices for arias that re-sounded in the summer night sky and al-most caused the ancient columns to split and held the audience spellbound. Since then concerts are held here every sum-mer, now at a safe distance from the dec-orative and crumbling ruins of the ancient Baths where once 1500 bathers could as-semble at a time. In the summer months, you can enjoy performances here by the *Teatro dell'Opera. Mon 9am–1pm, Tue–Sun 9am to one hour before sunset | ad-mission 11 euros | Via delle Terme di Cara-calla 52 | Metro B Circo Massimo | bus 628*

TRIPS

CASTELLI ROMANI (155 E5–6) *(ⱷ 0)*

The villages and small towns of the *castelli romani*, the roman castles, are situated on what must be the world's oldest wine rou-te. Caesar and Brutus had villas in *Frasca-ti* (approx. 20 km/12.4 mi south of Rome) in the Alban Hills. The Baroque residence of Cardinal Aldobrandini is not open to vi-sitors, but you can see its park and *Teat-ro dell'Acqua*. What attracts most daytrip-pers is the delicious white Frascati wine to go with suckling pig, *porchetta*, eaten at a market stall. *Zaraza (closed Mon, and Sun evening in winter | Viale Regina Margher-ita 45 | tel. 0 69 42 20 53 | Moderate)* is a popular place to eat and drink on the pa-noramic route.

On the ☟ route to *Castel Gandolfo* you have a wonderful view of a volcanic lake, *Lago di Nemi*, where there are paths for walkers. The best-known resident of Cas-tel Gandolfo was Pope Benedict XVI. Since 2014, the *Giardino Barberini (guid-ed tours Mon–Sat 8.30 and 11.30am | ad-mission 26 euros | www.vatican.va)*, the papal park, as well as parts of the sum-mer residence can be visited by groups (pre-booking required). At the *Hosteria* *la Fraschetta (closed Mon | Via della Re-pubblica 58 | tel. 0 69 36 13 12 | Budget)* you can still get home-made pasta, for example *fettuccine* with ceps, for a mere 10 euros! *Directions: from the orbital mo-torway Grande Raccordo Anulare (G.R.A.), motorway A1 or N215 to Frascati or N7 to Castel Gandolfo; by train: from Termini to Frascati or Castel Gandolfo; bus: between Frascati and Castel Gandolfo blue Cotral buses run about every 30 min.*

CERVETERI (154 A3) *(ⱷ 0)*

At a time when Rome was little more than a village, the Etruscan city of *Caere*, now Cerveteri (44 km/27.3 mi north-west of Rome) was one of the largest in the Mediterranean region with 100,000 inhabitants. The Etruscan ne-cropolises are a little bit outside the cen-tre. The activities of *tombaroli*, grave robbers, fortunately spared the *Tomba degli Alari*, the grave of a woman that was discovered in 1905 with a full set of household goods, jewellery and bot-tles of perfume.

Of the eight graves in the *Necropoli di Banditaccia* that are open to visitors, the *Tomba dei Rilievi (Tue–Sun 8.30am–7pm, in winter till 4pm | admission 8 euros)*, the "tomb of the reliefs" with its stuc-co decoration is undoubtedly the most impressive. The grave goods, weapons and cult items found here are on display in the *Museo Nazionale Cerite (Tue–Sun 8.30am–7pm | admission 8 euros, with the Nekropoli 10 euros)* in *Castello Rus-poli*, a Renaissance palace on Piazza S. Maria in Cerveteri. *Directions: Cervet-eri, motorway A12 or SS1 Via Aurelia; by train: local train to Ladispoli (direction of Grosseto, approx. one every hour) from Stazione Termini, change to a blue Cotral bus for Cerveteri, then a one-hour walk to the necropolises, in summer a shuttle bus | www.comune.cerveteri.rm.it*

TIVOLI (155 F3) (*ⓜ 0*)

It is like a world exhibition of antiquity! *Villa Adriana (daily 9am until one hour before dusk | admission 8 euros)*, to be found just before you get to Tivoli, almost 30 km/ 18.6 mi east of Rome, is surrounded by oaks, pines and cypresses. Fascinated by the impressions he had gained on his travels through the whole Roman Empire, Emperor Hadrian (76–138 AD) built a palace where he could show the highlights of Roman civilisation to his visitors: the Lyceum and Stoa Poikile, the gate of the agora in Athens, large and small baths, the valley of temples in Thessaly and the Nile canal between Alexandria and Canopus.

The emperor spent his hours of leisure in the bizarre Teatro Marittimo, a temple on an island between his hall of philosophers and a Greek and Latin library. Perhaps he was mourning his beautiful young friend Antinous, who died young and whose statues adorn every corner of the residence.

In the town of Tivoli lies *Villa d'Este (Tue–Sun 8.30am until one hour before dusk | admission 8 euros | Piazza Villa d'Este 1)* with its amazing water features, which are fed by the *fontana dell'organo idraulico*, a spectacular "water organ". Cardinal Ippolito (1509–72) had this terrace-like Renaissance park with its 500 springs and fountains built at the foot of his sumptuous villa. *Directions: take Via Tiburtina, Settecamini to the place called Villa Adriana. By bus: blue Cotral bus from Metro B: Ponte Mammolo to Villa Adriana, 15 min on foot to Hadrian's villa, then a short walk to the C. A.T. bus (shuttle) to Tivoli Centro. 5 min to Villa d'Este. Return: Cotral bus to Metro B: Ponte Mammolo | www.comune.tivoli.rm.it.*

The town of Tivoli with the fountains of Villa d'Este makes a great day trip

FOOD & DRINK

Cucina romana is plain food: regional, seasonal and original. Nothing is prepared without high quality native olive oil (olio d'oliva extra vergine).

The art lies in the fresh ingredients: tomatoes, which taste like tomatoes, dozens of lettuce varieties and wild vegetables like thistles and artichokes that the Roman Emperors already enjoyed. This is served with hearty meat dishes like lamb (abbacchio) or offal, but this is not a must. Everyone eats as much vegetarian/vegan food as he likes. And pasta, of course. It's funny, but true: pasta and delicatessen stores offer more choice and variety than toy shops. The pasta alphabet ranges from A for agnolotti, meat-filled pasta parcels, to S, the twisted strozzapreti, "priest-stranglers", or T for tagliolini, a kind of ribbon pasta. In Rome, molecular cuisine or the paleo diet have no chance. "We Romans don't need to follow any trends and fashion because we're legends in our own right", claims Antonello Colonna, Chef de Cuisine at the "Open Colonna", situated on the roof terrace of the Palazzo delle Esposizioni, and overlooking the city and so rising above things. Another legend was Lucius Lucullus, a Roman general during Caesar's day, who won a place in history not with the military but as a gourmet and champion banqueter.

Food is still a favourite pastime for most Italians who savour their food. But breakfast or colazione, which is usually enjoyed standing in a bar, is a brief affair: a single caffè or a cappuccino, including

Roman cuisine follows a simple recipe: the best is just good enough, and it flourishes right here

croissant on the way to the office are sufficient. And for lunch or *pranzo,* (usually between 1pm and 3pm), which once included several courses, nowadays you will be able to get away with ordering just a starter *(primo)* and a salad, and you can leave out the main course *(secondo).* In the evening the Roman restaurants are often fully booked, so it is better to reserve a table – or arrive early. Most restaurants already open at 7.30pm. You should have plenty of time: in the evenings at good restaurants it is usual to eat several courses plus *dolce,* a sweet dessert.

Salute! When it comes to drinking, Italians are traditionally-minded. To accompany a meal they usually order a light house wine *(vino sfuso/vino di casa),* which will be good and cheap – and, it goes without saying, dry. A DOC or DOCG sign on the label is a guarantee of the origin by region or location. White wines made nearby in Castelli Romani, e.g. Frascati, are popular, as is a glass of fresh-tasting Orvieto, Vernaccia di San Gimignano and dry Verdicchio.

Café with statues: be inspired in the former studio of the sculptor Canova

There is no real equivalent to the pub in Italy. The restaurant proprietor will look askance if you just order beer but no food. In a pizzeria too, you shuold order at least a snack. If you like wine, an alternative is going to a *vinoteca,* a wine bar.

Italians make a little ritual about paying for a meal. The waiter brings the bill (il conto) – 15 per cent service is usually included – and brings back exact change down to the last cent. If you were satisfied, you leave up to five per cent on the plate. Unfortunately standards of service and courtesy have fallen noticeably in recent years, especially in the tourist zones. Another tip: ask for an official bill *(ricevuta fiscale),* as tax inspectors sometimes make checks.

CAFÉS & ICE-CREAM PARLOURS

INSIDER TIP ATELIER CANOVA TADOLINI ● (147 E4) (⫿ E6)
In what was once the studio of the sculptor and architect Antonio Canova you can enjoy your cappuccino or aperitif between fine works in plaster and marble. But of course they are copies. Even a trip to the WC holds artistic surprises in store. This is a popular stop-off near the Spanish Steps. *Mon–Sat 8am–11pm, Sun 10am–11pm | Via del Babuino 150 | www.canovatadolini.com | Metro A Spagna*

CAFFETERIA CHIOSTRO DEL BRAMANTE ★ (144 B–C3) (⫿ D8)
On a terrace above the elegant Renaissance courtyard built by Bramante you can enjoy coffee or brunch (Sun from 11am), have an aperitif from 5pm, browse in the bookshop and view an exhibition. From the ✂ *Sala delle Sibille* on the first floor you can also look at a highlight of the neighbouring church of *Santa Maria della Pace* (see p. 46) which is seldom open: frescoes of the sibyls painted by Raphael. *Mon–Fri 10am–8pm, Sat/Sun 10am–9pm | Arco della Pace 5 | www.chiostrodelbramante.it | bus 40, 62, 64*

CAMBIOVITA ⊘ (144 B4) (*ⅢⅡ D8*)

The name of this small café says it all: CamBIOvita! All dishes and ice creams are either vegetarian or vegan. *Daily 8am–11pm | Via del Governo Vecchio 54/44 | bus 40, 60, 62, 64*

INSIDER **TIP** **GINGER** ⊘

(145 E1) (*ⅢⅡ E7*)

In this organic bistro and café situated on the exclusive Via Borgognona, health-conscious Romans sip their smoothies, organic fruit juices, herbal teas and even a good old cappuccino from time to time. *Daily 10am–midnight | Via Borgognona 43–44 | bus 62, 63 | Metro A Spagna*

GELATERIA GIOLITTI ●

(145 D2–3) (*ⅢⅡ E8*)

Rome's most famous ice-cream salon has been in business since 1900. The selection is stunning. Traditionalists order the *bacio* chocolate ice cream or the truffle ice. Fruit sorbets, champagne flavour and ginger are also chart-toppers here. It's the haunt of half the members of the Italian parliament. *Daily 7–2am | Via Uffici del Vicario 40 | www.giolitti.it | bus 62, 63*

GREZZO RAW CHOCOLATE ⊘

(148 B6) (*ⅢⅡ G6*)

Raw chocolate – is that the sweetest organic promise ever? On the Via Urbana at least ice cream fans stand in a queue. At Grezzo they think they have discovered the egg of Columbus, that is, the "evolution of healthy sweets". Ice cream and chocolates, truffles and cakes – everything in the store is made from raw chocolate. The unprocessed cocoa ingredient should contain the original nutrients and is a rich source of anti-oxidants. No bad conscience next time you eat ice cream! In the trendy Monti quarter. *Daily 11am–11pm | Via Urbana 130 | www.grezzoitalia.it | Metro B Cavou*

INSIDER **TIP** **GROM** ⊘ (144 C3) (*ⅢⅡ D8*)

Two young Turinese had the perfect slow-food ice idea, grew their own organic fruit on their plantations in Piedmont – and voila: a new super-gelato was born. Insider tip: cantaloupe melon! Also situated near the Pantheon *(Via della Maddalena 30)*. *Sun–Thu 11–1am, Fri/Sat 11–1.30am | Piazza Navona 1 | bus 40, 64, 70, 81, 492*

MARCO POLO HIGHLIGHTS

★ **Caffetteria Chiostro del Bramante**
Coffee and art in the cloister courtyard → p. 72

★ **Checchino dal 1887**
The international elite dines here in the slaughterhouse quarter → p. 75

★ **Il San Lorenzo**
Fish, fish and more fish around the corner from Campo de' Fiori → p. 76

★ **Pierluigi**
Eat lusciously on Piazza Ricci with a sparkling prosecco for aperitif → p. 76

★ **Sciuè Sciuè**
Young Roman cuisine served in a pleasant atmosphere in Monti → p. 80

★ **Pommidoro**
Trattoria, old-fashioned style, where not only artists come to dine → p. 77

SAID-ANTICA FABBRICA DEL CIOCCOLATO ● (149 E6) (*Ⓜ K8*)

In this old chocolate factory dating from 1923 in San Lorenzo you can try and buy the creations of the chocolatiers (ricotta-filled chocolates are delicious). While sitting in a café on trendy barstools made of milk chums, drink a hot chocolate, whose milk is so frothy, the spoon stands upright. The cooks ensure that every served meal is in tune with chocolate. *Tue–Sun 10–1am | Via Tiburtina 135/ Via Marrucini | tel. 0 64 46 92 04 | www.said. it | tram/bus 3, 19*

SANT'EUSTACHIO (145 D4) (*Ⓜ E8*)

The aroma emanating from Rome's oldest coffee roasting establishment wafts over Piazza Sant'Eustachio, where other cafés that roast their own beans have set up shop. The *caffè* comes already sweetened unless you order it "senza zucchero". *Daily 8.30–1am | Piazza Sant'Eustachio 82 | bus 75*

SCIASCIA CAFFÈ (146 C4) (*Ⓜ C6*)

You might almost have walked past it! The historic café dating from 1919 has no tables outside, but inside it looks like the cosy and elegant Belle Époque Viennese coffee houses. The green upholstered armchairs, vintage sofa and panelled walls are inviting, and the cappuccino – one of the best in Rome – is served in small porcelain cups by Riccardo Ginori. The café, which is a favourite with young lawyers, doctors and legal clerks, is situated in the Prati quarter near the

FAVOURITE EATERIES

"Green Bar" – literally

The small restaurant 🌐 *Aromaticus Green Bar* (148 B6) (*Ⓜ G8–9*) *(Tue–Sun 10am–9pm | Via Urbana 134 | tel. 0 64 88 13 55 | www.aromaticus.it | Metro B Cavour | Moderate)* is decorated from top to bottom with green materials – from flower seeds and herb pots from a caper plant to sugar snaps or peppers. Guests cannot only savour the aromas, but also buy the plants for their window seat back home. Luca and Francesca are members of the *urban farming* community that cultivates vegetable gardens on rooftop terraces. Try the original and small slow food dishes and soups, tartare or beef carpaccio with plenty of vegetables and herb variations for approx. 10 euros. All dishes are available as takeaways.

Dinner in the railway bistro?

It doesn't sound that exciting. But when two Michelin star chef **INSIDERTIP** ▶ *Oliver Glowig* (148 C6) (*Ⓜ H8–9*) *(daily 12 noon–9pm | Mercato Centrale in Termini railway station | entrance Via Giolitti 36 | tel. 06 92 94 99 16 | www.oliverglowig. com | Metro A, B Termini | Moderate)* recently opened a restaurant in the hectic Termini railway station, it was a big hit. Fortunately, for all ordinary visitors the prices have drastically fallen, but the creativity is the same. No main dish costs more than 20 euros. Try the *lush tonno spada* or Glowig's trademark *eliche, cacio, pepe e ricci di mare*, spiral pasta with cheese and fresh sea urchins. The bistro – its name is "Il Tavolo, il Vino e la Dispensa", but nobody calls it that – also sells wine, cheese and 🌐 finest organic ingredients.

Three-star German chef Heinz Beck impresses guests at the La Pergola restaurant in Rome

Vatican. *Daily 7am–8pm | Via Fabio Via Massimo 80 | www.sciascia1919.com | Metro A Ottaviano/San Pietro or Lepanto*

RESTAURANTS: EXPENSIVE

ANTONELLO COLONNA – OPEN
(148 A–B6) (*ⓜ G8*)

Inside the gourmet restaurant on the rooftop terrace of the Palazzo delle Esposizioni, the décor is cool and modern. Try the *tortelli* with foie gras, *cappeletti* with scampi, squid with potatoes or pigeon with *polenta*. Incidentally, the Open Colonna is also multifunctional: at lunchtime, you can sample the *City Lunch* (Tue–Sat 12.30pm–3.30pm) with a superb vegetarian buffet for 16 euros, while on weekends *Brunch is popular (Sat/Sun 12.30pm–3.30pm | 30 euros per person)* and large Roman families come out to

dine. *Gourmet restaurant: Tue–Sat from 7pm reservation only | Via Milano 9a | tel. 06 47 82 26 41 | www.antonellocolonna. it.open | bus 64, 70, 170*

CHECCHINO DAL 1887 ★
(151 D5) (*ⓜ D12*)

This upscale trattoria, which serves hearty Roman food, attracts a high-ranking international clientele. Its specialities are dishes using innards. The wine list is excellent. *Tue–Sat | Via Monte Testaccio 30 | tel. 06 57 43 8 16 | www.checchino-dal-1887.com | bus 170*

LA PERGOLA 〰️ (146 A1) (*ⓜ A3*)

Well, he is the King of Rome! Heinz Beck, who was voted as top chef for the first time in 1997, has three Michelin stars. The nine-course menu on the rooftop terrace of the luxury hotel Cavalieri

The genuine article: parmiggiano reggiano in the gourmet palace Eataly

Waldorf Astoria with views of Rome and celebrities is a snip at 220 euros. *Tue–Sat evenings only | Via Alberto Cadlolo 101 | tel. 06 35 09 1 | www. romecavalieri.it | bus 907, 913*

PIERLUIGI ★ (144 B4) (*Ø C–D 8–9*)

You have a wonderful position here on the romantic Piazza dei Ricci. The fish, spaghetti in langoustine sauce, carpaccio and chocolate cake are famous locally. Try the dry house Prosecco, Bernabei, for a bit of sparkle with your meal. Rather high-priced. *Tue–Sun | Piazza de' Ricci 144 | tel. 06 68 68 71 7 | tel. 06 68 68 13 02 | bus 64*

IL SAN LORENZO ★ (144 C5) (*Ø D9*)

Not all fish are the same. The San Lorenzo restaurant near Campo de'Fiori serves the finest tuna fish, bream, sea urchins and scampi carpaccio. Excellent wine list, expensively priced. *Mon–Sat | Via dei Chiavari 4 | tel. 06 68 65 09 7 | www.ilsanlorenzo.it | bus 40, 62, 64, 116*

LA VERANDA (146 C5) (*Ø B7*)

Do you recognize the room with the colourful frescoes from Paolo Sorrentino's cult film "La Grande Bellezza"? Or the tall window bays and flickering torches in the intimate courtyard? The 15th century Cardinal's palace is still filled with the atmosphere of the Renaissance and offers the finest youthful and creative cuisine – e.g. squid with smoked aubergine, braised veal with apple sauce and lamb's lettuce or *orecchiette* with scampi and chicory salad. *Tue–Sun | Via della Conciliazione 33 | Hotel Columbus | tel. 06 68 72 97 3 | www.laveranda.net | bus 40, 62*

RESTAURANTS: MODERATE

INSIDER TIP ANTICA HOSTARIA L'ARCHEOLOGIA (155 D5) (*∅ K–L16*)
If you are looking for a nice garden restaurant after a dusty walk on Via Appia Antica, this is it! Wisteria and roses bloom, little fountains gurgle and the pasta dishes, e.g. with fish and mussels, are just superb. *Daily | Via Appia Antica 139 | tel. 0 67 88 04 94 | bus 118*

INSIDER TIP EATALY ◐
(151 F6) (*∅ F13–14*)
A gourmet palace spread over two floors, where you can choose between a range of 23 slow-food restaurants and stands with delicacies and stock up on the finest olive oils, organic wines, hundreds of different types of pasta and cookbooks. *Daily 10am–midnight | ex-air terminal Ostiense | Piazzale 12 Octobre 1492 | www. roma.eataly.it | bus 60, 95, 121, 175, 280 Piazzale di Partigiani (badly signposted) | Metro B Piramide (300 m through an underpass to Stazione Ostiense)*

DA FELICE (151 E5) (*∅ E12*)
Always a busy and welcoming location. The restaurateur apparently serves the city's best *spaghetti carbonara* or *tonnarelli cacio e pepe*. The famous slogan is, "Our dishes have stayed the same since 1936". Some Romans see it as winning the lottery if they land a table at this eatery (reservation by phone only)! *Daily | Via Mastro Giorgio 29/Via Galvani | tel. 0 65 74 68 00 | www.feliceatestaccio. it | Metro B Piramide | bus 83, 121, 673*

GINA (145 E1) (*∅ E7*)
Gina's is actually a high-class snack bar serving sandwiches of salmon and beef or swordfish carpaccio. But the real sensation here is **INSIDER TIP** Gina's picnic basket to take away to the nearby park of Villa Borghese: luxury rolls, red wine, cheese, fruit, coffee, corkscrew and tablecloth (approx. 40–65 euros). *Via San Sebastiano 7a | Piazza di Spagna | tel. 0 66 78 02 51 | www. ginaroma.com | Metro A Spagna*

POMMIDORO ★ (149 F6) (*∅ K8*)
The *letterati* Alberto Moravia and Pier Paolo Pasolini philosophised here over their *spaghetti all'amatriciana*. The landlord never cashed Pasolini's last cheque, which he wrote the evening before he died.
The artists and glitterati, the eccentric characters of San Lorenzo still meet here, because Anna and Aldo's food is so good. *Mon–Sat | Piazza dei Sanniti 44 | tel. 0 64 45 26 92 | tram/bus 3, 19*

CAFFÈ E GELATO

It's not essential to know these facts for a short break in Rome – but have you already heard that...
... When asked for an "Espresso", Romans think of an express train and not a shot of coffee, which is simply known as *caffè*?
... In the land of the *gelato*, you can never just order ice cream scoops, but only flavours (*gusti*), which cost 2, 3 or 4 euros?
... that Ferragosto on 15th August is a big family festival for all Italians which has already been celebrated since the days of Emperor Augustus?
... "Pizza" is one of the few Italian words understood almost world-wide? But the word originating from Greek *pita* probably comes from the Orient.

LOCAL SPECIALITIES

abbacchio alla scottadito – roast lamb with rosemary potatoes

baccalà – dried cod, often served with peas

bollito misto – mixed boiled meats, usually served with a green sauce

bucatini all'amatriciana – pasta with tomato sauce, bacon and pecorino

carciofi alla giudea/romana – artichokes fried in oil

carpaccio di manzo – thin raw slices of fillet of beef with rocket leaves and Parmesan

carpaccio di pesce – thin marinated slices of swordfish or tuna (photo right)

ciammotta – deep-fried vegetables

coniglio alla cacciatora – rabbit braised in the oven with rosemary

fave e pecorino – beans with pecorino

finanziera – stew of chicken, sweetbread and mushrooms

garofolato – braised beef

insalata di puntarelle – bitter salad leaves with garlic and anchovies

orecchiette – ear-shaped pasta, often served with broccoli and scampi

ortiche – young nettles as a creamy pasta sauce

pagliata – calf's intestines with penne

panzanella – white bread with tomatoes, oil and chopped basil as a salad

panzarottini – filled pasta baked with cheese and egg

pasta e fagioli – penne or other fresh pasta with bean soup

pesce spada – swordfish with lemon and oil, usually grilled

pollo al diavolo – spicy chicken

porchetta – slices of suckling pig on a roll, usually served cold at a stall (photo left)

saltimbocca – slice of veal with sage and Parma ham

scamorza con prosciutto – smoked cheese with ham

trippa alla romana – tripe, usually served with vegetables

PORTO FLUVIALE (151 E6) (*E13*)
This beautiful old warehouse is the new place to be seen in Testaccio/Ostiense. *Trattoria*, *birreria*, grill bar, buffet, bar, lounge all in one. INSIDER TIP Mon–Fri large lunchtime buffet for 10 euros. *Daily 10.30am–2pm | Via Porto Fluviale 22 | www.portofluviale.com | Metro B Piramide | bus 23, 83, 271, 673*

RESTAURANTS: BUDGET

DA AUGUSTO ● (151 D2) *(🕮 D10)*

One of Trastevere's good old trattorias. You are sitting on the *piazza* and more often than not Augusto, the host, will personally set the paper tablecloth and immediately take your order. If you can't understand his thick accent, simply order the dish of the day from the blackboard, e.g. *coniglio* (rabbit) or *pollo* (chicken). *Closed Sat evenings and Sun | Piazza de' Renzi 15 | tel. 0 65 80 37 98 | tram 8*

IL BOCCONCINO ◍ (152 B2) *(🕮 G10)*

Right behind the Colosseum, Nelly and Giancarlo – who is actually a pharmacist– have opened a slow-food trattoria that has become a real hit in the locality. Try their traditional Roman-style starters such as *polpette di melanzane e pinoli*, aubergine dumplings with pine kernels, crostini di alici, toasted bread with anchovies, or *spezzatino di vitella,* veal stew with beans. *Thu–Tue | Via Ostilia 23 | tel. 06 77 07 91 75 | Metro B Colosseo | bus 75, 81, 85, 117 | tram 3*

ENZO AL 29 (151 E3) *(🕮 E10)*

The tiny trattoria tucked away in a small alley in Trastevere has just a few wobbly tables outside on the cobblestones. If you're lucky enough to have reserved a table for the evening, you should arrive promptly! After ten minutes, Enzo gives the table to the next in line. Meanwhile, Enzo, Giulia and Francesco serve all those waiting with a glass of wine. Despite the overdone hype, it's good: lasagne with pine nuts, pumpkin flowers stuffed with Mozzarella and anchovies and *rigatoni alla matriciana. Tue–Sun 12.30pm–3pm and 7.30pm–10pm | Via dei Vascellari 29/Via dei Genovesi | tel. 0 65 81 22 60 | www. daenzoal29.com | tram 8*

Typical Roman food, served on Campo de' Fiori: Hostaria Romanesca

DA FRANCO AR VICOLETTO
(149 E6) (*K8*)

For 30 years Franco's regulars in the university and workers' quarter of San Lorenzo have been coming here – originally as students, now accompanied by their children. A three-course menu costs 30 euros, **INSIDER TIP** starter and main course can be had for 20 euros. *Tue–Sun | Via dei Falisci 3 | tel. 06 49 57 67 5 | bus 71*

DA GIOVANNI
(144 A6) (*C9*)

You have to get here early, as this simple little osteria, one of the last of its kind, is very popular with the artisans and other residents of the area. The pasta is of course home-made, and all the wines are sold by the glass or carafe. *Mon–Sat | Via della Lungara 41a | tel. 06 68 61 51 4 | bus 23, 280*

HOSTARIA ROMANESCA
(144 C5) (*D9*)

Come for the view alone! You are sitting on the sunny side of life here on buzzing, colourful Campo de' Fiori. No sophisticated cooking, just plain Roman dishes like *spaghetti carbonara* and *pollo ai peperoni*. A reservation is necessary in the evenings! *Daily | Campo de' Fiori 40 | tel. 06 68 62 02 4 | bus 116*

SCIUÈ SCIUÈ ★
(152 B1) (*G9*)

In Neapolitan *sciuè sciuè* means light and casual. This suits this attractive café-restaurant in Monti where Francesco creates a new menu every day with fresh vegetables, fish and pasta at affordable prices. Dishes include baked courgette flowers or tuna fish tartar with oranges and pine nuts. *Daily | Via Urbana 56–57 | tel. 06 48 90 60 38 | www.sciuesciueroma.com | Metro B Cavour | bus 117*

SERGIO ALLE GROTTE
(144 C5) (*D9*)

This wonderfully old-fashioned trattoria is hidden away in an alley off Via Giubbonari behind Campo de' Fiori. Try Sergio's classics such as *spaghetti amatriciana or puttanesca*. There's fresh fish on Tuesdays, Fridays and Saturdays. *Mon–Sat | Vicolo delle Grotte 27 | tel. 06 86 42 93 | tram 8 | bus 30, 40, 62, 63, 64*

TRAM TRAM
(149 F6) (*L8*)

The name derives from the tram that passes on its way to Porta Maggiore. The cooking is Roman with Sicilian and Pugliese influences e.g. *orechiette alla Norma*, ear-shaped pasta with vegetables, *rigatoni alla pajatina* with calf's intestines, and *gnocchi con baccalà*, i.e. with cod. *Tue–Sun | Via dei Reti 46 |*

LOW BUDGET

Enjoy your *caffè* or juice at the bar counter. At tables – especially near tourist attractions – it's often three times as expensive.

You can get a quick refreshment or cup of coffee for very little money at the bar next to the souvenir stand run by nuns in the dome of *San Pietro* **(146 B5) (*A7*)**.

At a delicatessen store, e.g. at *Volpetti* **(147 E5) (*D–E7*)** *(Via della Scrofa 31)* you get a decent pasta dish for about 8 euros.

A gastronomic delight close to St. Peters' Square: *FaFaMi Laboratorio Gastronomico* **(146 C5) (*C7*)** *(Mon–Sat 9.30am–5pm | Via degli Ombrelari 7/Borgo Pio)* serves delicious antipasti and snacks for under 8 euros.

tel. 06 49 04 16 | www.tramtram.it | tram 3, 19 | bus 492

VINOTECHE (WINE BARS)

BUCCONE (147 E4) (*∅ E6*)

Where horses were stabled once, exquisite wines are stored today. Enjoy them with light dishes such as pasta and baked aubergines, and an array of high-quality olive oils and balsamic vinegars. *Mon–Thu only midday, Fri/Sat evenings too | Via di Ripetta 19–20 | tel. 06 36 12 15 4 | www.enotecabuccone.com | Metro A Flaminio*

VINI, VIZI E VIRTÙ (146 C4) (*∅ B–C6*)

"Wines, vices and virtues" is the name of this small, charming wine bar just five minutes away from the Vatican where Antonio Mazzitelli recommends excellent wines to his guests at decent prices. Popular spot for young Romans. *Mon–Sat | Piazza dell'Unità 15 | tel. 06 89 53 70 95 | Metro A Ottaviano-San Pietro | tram 19 | bus 81*

INSIDER TIP ► VINOROMA
(152 B1) (*∅ G9*)

With her guided Italian wine tastings, the sommelière Hande Leimer has created an iconic Roman experience, guiding you through seven Italian wines in her pretty flat in the old town (50 euros/person). *Daily by prior arrangement | Via in Selci 84/G | mobile tel. 32 84 87 44 97 | www.vinoroma.com | bus C3, 84, 75 | Metro B Cavour*

PIZZERIAS & TAVOLE CALDE (SNACK BUFFETS)

DA BAFFETTO (144 B3) (*∅ D8*)

An established institution close to Piazza Navona. Hungry customers queue here every evening. *Daily, evenings only | Via del Governo Vecchio 114 | tel. 06 86 16 17 | bus 40, 62, 64*

IL BOSCAIOLO (148 A4) (*∅ F7*)

Pizzeria north of the Fontana di Trevi with a wide selection of toppings and thin, crispy dough. The salads are good, too. *Tue–Sun | Via degli Artisti 37 | tel. 06 48 88 40 23 | Metro A Barberini*

A cappuccino is delicious but an insult to the café owner after a meal

ER BUCHETTO (148 B6) (*∅ G–H8*)

Three plain wooden tables and no choice at all: what Franco makes is genuine *porchetta*, a Roman pork dish seasoned with salt, pepper and fennel. The juicy roast is cooked on a rotating spit and eaten with white bread. From 5 euros per portion. *Mon–Sat 10am–3pm, 5pm–9pm | Via del Viminale 2f | Metro A/B B Termini Cavour | bus 40, 64*

ALLE FRATTE DI TRASTEVERE
(151 D3) (*∅ D10*)

Crispy pizzas and simple Roman cuisine, friendly service. Situated at the heart of the trendy district Trastevere, this old pizzeria has remained unchanged and affordable. *Thu–Tue | Via delle Fratte di Trastevere 49–50 | next to Ospedale San Gallicano | tel. 06 58 35 75 | tram H, 8*

SHOPPING

CITY **WHERE TO START?**
A good start for shopping is the bus stop on **Largo Chigi/Piazza San Silvestro, (145 E2) (🚇 E7)** at the start of the pedestrian zone. From here you are within easy reach of the exclusive shops between Via Frattina, Via Condotti and Via Borgognona continuing to Piazza di Spagna, but you can also stroll along the much cheaper Via del Corso. *Metro A Spagna | bus 52, 53, 61, 62, 63, 71, 80, 85, 95, 175, 492*

The shopping A to Z of *alta moda* ranges from Armani to Zegna, from **Laura Biagiotti to Valentino** – these are slightly more mature designers whose boutiques and flagship stores are in the chic inner-city palazzi.

Here, you're at the source: the Piazza di Spagna with Gucci, Prada, Versace, Dolce & Gabbana and the jeweller Bulgari look like the centrefold of "Vogue" magazine. The Via Condotti and Via Borgognona seduce the clientele – those wearing the trousers and with plenty of money – to indulge in a stylish shopping bonanza. It's at least worth a glimpse of the elegant shopping gallery on the corner of the Via del Corso/Via del Tritone: ● *Galleria Alberto Sordi* with cafés and boutiques.

Monti is an excellent address for bargain hunters and vintage collectors. You will also find original retro and second-hand stores in the Via del Governo Vecchio or

Alta moda (high fashion) in the palazzi, funky artisan pieces, vintage and retro in the small side streets – Italian design is unrivalled

Via dei Banchi Nuovi towards the River Tiber. Handmade handbags or belts in all colours are now also offered in small shops around the Pantheon or near the Campo de' Fiori. As well as fashion, don't forget gourmet ingredients. Rome's food markets like Piazza San Cosimato or the numerous small *alimentari,* the delicatessen, offer appetizing souvenirs to take back home like Parmigiano, olive oil or Parma ham.

Many shops are open from 10am to 8pm, but some close between 1pm and 4 or 5pm in the summer heat. In winter everything stays closed on Monday morning – except the food shops.

ORGANIC FOOD STORES & MARKETS

ALBERO DEL PANE ⊙ (145 D5) (⌂ E9) Rome's oldest health-food shop has all kinds of organic foodstuffs, juices, vegetables and environmentally sound washing powders and detergents, as well as a big range of natural cosmetics. *Via San-*

ta Maria del Pianto 19–20 | www.roma biologica.com | tram 8 | bus H, 30, 63, 780

ANTICA ERBORISTERIA ROMANA 🌐
(145 D4) (𝄞 E8–9)

Dating back to 1752, Rome's oldest herbal pharmacy has always offered alternative medicines. Beautiful woodwork features. *Via di Torre Argentina 15 | bus 40, 62, 64*

fruit, vegetables, honey, cheese, wine and olive oil. The nearby Campo de' Fiori also transforms into an organic oasis every third Sunday in the month. *2nd and 4th Sun, 9am–5pm | Vicolo della Moretta | bus 62, 64 | tram 8*

DIMENSIONE NATURA 🌐
(145 D5) (𝄞 C8)

This fashion shop near the Fontana delle

Rome's oldest herbal pharmacy: Antica Erboristeria Romana has always supplied alternative medicines

ORGANIC MARKET AT THE SLAUGHTERHOUSE 🌐
(151 D5) (𝄞 D12–13)

The green space at the *mattatoio*, the former slaughterhouse is a green oasis. Every Sunday from 10am–5pm organic farmers sell their fresh vegetables, olive oil, honey and homemade pasta. *Piazza Orazio Giustiniani 4 | bus 23, 280*

ORGANIC MARKET DELLA MORETTA 🌐
(144 B4) (𝄞 C8)

Twice a month organic farmers from the surrounding area sell their products:

Tartarughe on Piazza Mattei aims to combine ecological textiles made from cashmere, alpaca, linen and silk with chic Roman style. *Via dei Falegnami 66a | www. dimensionenatura.eu | tram 8 | bus 30, 40, 63, 64, 70*

PEPERITA E IL CAVALLINO 🌐
(145 D5) (𝄞 E9)

Organic farmer Rita Salvadori grows hundreds of different types of chilli peppers on her estate, her sister Romina is in charge of the olive trees and produces the prize-winning olive oil "Il Cavallino".

Both products are available from the shop in the ghetto at Piazza Mattei. *Via della Reginella 30 | www.ilcavallino.it | www. peperita.it | tram 8*

German and Spanish. *Via della Lungaretta 23 | www.books-in-italy.com | tram 8 | bus H*

BOOKSHOPS

FELTRINELLI

Publishing house with three modern bookshops and an excellent range of international literature. *Galleria Alberto Sordi 33* | (147 F5) *(* D *E8) Metro A Spagna; Via E. Orlando 84* | (148 B5) *(* D *G7 | Metro A Repubblica; also Sun 10am–9pm; Largo di Torre Argentina 11* | (145 D4) *(* D *E9)* | *bus 62, 64*

OPEN DOOR BOOKSHOP

(151 D–E2) *(* D *E10)*

They are gradually becoming hard to find. Since Herder closed near the parliament, now Rome only has a handful of international bookstores. But this welcoming bookshop in Trastevere has kept going for forty years. Most are second-hand books in Italian, English,

FINE FOODS

ANTICA CACIARA TRASTEVERINA ◈
(151 D3) *(* D *D10)*

So you think that cheese couldn't run away from you? On Saturdays, make sure you don't arrive late at the 100-year-old delicatessen shop, otherwise the fresh sheep's or goat's ricotta cheese or real *mozzarella di bufala*, from the buffalo, will be sold out. You can console yourself with Sardinian *pecorino*, different varieties of salami or San Daniele hams that foodies prefer to fine Parma ham. *Via San Francesco a Ripa 140 | www.anticacaciara.it | tram 8 | bus H*

ANTICA SALUMERIA (145 D3) *(* D *E8)*

Delicacies such as sheep's and goat's cheese, Parma ham, olives, top wines and delicious pizza. Piazza della Rotonda 3/Pantheon | bus 40, 62, 64, 81

⭐ **Aldo Fefe**
Old-style stationer and bookbinder → **p. 87**

⭐ **Interiors 32**
Lamps and lighting from the swinging fifties → **p. 86**

⭐ **Nora P**
Design accessories, artificial flower arrangements and furniture → **p. 86**

⭐ **Porta Portese**
Sunday flea market in Trastevere – a genuine Roman institution → **p. 88**

⭐ **Cucinelli**
Finest cashmere, exclusive prices, social conscience: Brunello Cucinelli → **p. 88**

⭐ **Ibiz Artigianato di Cuoio**
Handbags, handmade in every colour → **p. 89**

⭐ **Gucci**
Bags large and small and accessories by the luxury brand → **p. 89**

⭐ **Sermoneta Gloves**
Available here: elegant leather gloves for Signora and Signore → **p. 90**

MARCO POLO HIGHLIGHTS

INSIDER TIP ▶ ENOTECA ANTICA
(145 E1) (𝄐 E7)

A distinguished shop dating from 1905 selling vintage champagne, red and white wine and rare liqueurs. You can try the wines and eat a snack. *Via della Croce 76b | Metro A Spagna*

FOCACCI
(145 E1) (𝄐 E7)

Focacci stocks treats like dried ceps, truffles, olive oil, wine and grappa. *Via della Croce 45 | Metro A Spagna*

ITALIA DEL GUSTO 🌐
(144 C2) (𝄐 D7)

Delicate fig mustard, truffle sauce, matured ham, cheese, organic olive oil, the finest italian products, also suitable for presents. *Via dell'Orso 71 | bus 81, 492*

VOLPETTI (151 E4–4) (𝄐 E12)

Rome's chefs come here to buy excellent ingredients: a full range of Italian cheeses and hams, olive oil of the finest quality. At the counter you can eat a refined snack at midday. *Via Marmorata 47 | Metro B Piramide | bus 8, 23, 30, 75, 280 | tram 3*

DESIGN & HOME

ARTEMIDE (147 F4) (𝄐 E6)

From Tolomeo table lamps to Alfiere hanging lumieres in silver and the Arcadia bedside lamp – at Artemide's they are switched on to the latest trends. *Via Margutta 107 | www.artemide.com | Metro A Spagna*

BOSCHETTO TRE (148 B6) (𝄐 G8)

Mobiles with butterflies, dragonfly magnets, dog face cushions, stylish light bulbs, rugs made of recycled materials: the designer Oriana Tombolesi splendidly combines all different kinds of material. *Via Boschetto 3 | www.boschettotre.it | Metro A Spagna*

INTERIORS 32 ⭐ (147 E–F4) (𝄐 E6)

The swinging fifties have returned in this store with its collection of lamps and furniture: lamps from Gaetano Sciolari or the stage lighting instrument by Mole-Richardson. *Via dei Greci 32 | bus 117, 119*

MAURIZIO GROSSI (147 F4) (𝄐 E6)

Venus de Milo, busts of Caesars or an obelisk for your living room? Copies of artworks from antiquity, decorative and conveniently sized. *Via Margutta 109 | www.mauriziogrossi.com | Metro A Spagna*

NORA P ⭐ (152 A1) (𝄐 G8)

A stylish bathtub filled with flowering orchids or colourful deckchairs to brighten up your front room. Nora Pastore's design store brings new ideas even to trendy

Anything second-hand, clothes and lots of kitsch: Porta Portese flea market

Monti. *Via Panisperna 220–221 | www. nora-p.com | Metro B Cavour | bus 117*

GIFTS

ALDO FEFE ⭐ (145 D2) *(𝄞 E7)*
This shop for classy stationery and book-binding has been in business since 1932. Aldo, the owner, produces your personal books, albums or frames within two days. *Via della Stelletta 20b | bus 62, 64, 81, 87*

INSIDER TIP BOTTEGA DEL MARMORARO (147 F4) *(𝄞 E6)*
It's worth just visiting the workshop, and the old sculptor, Sandro Fiorentini, is charming. If he isn't just working on his marble statues, Sandro will gladly carve your name or favourite saying on a marble tablet that you can collect the next day (from 15 euros). And in Roman cuneiform script like in "Asterix Conquers Rome". The opening hours for the master workshop are flexible, he is

usually there Tue–Sat 9am–7.30pm. *Via Margutta 53b | Metro A Spagna*

CAMPO MARZIO DESIGN
(145 D2) *(𝄞 E7)*
Fountain pens and notebooks made from top-quality leather. *Via di Campo Marzio 41 | www.campomarziodesign.it | bus 116, 117*

INSIDER TIP TECH IT EASY
(145 E2) *(𝄞 E8)*
Everything the digital heart desires: clocks that show all time zones, unusual bathroom scales, electronic knick-knacks. *Via del Gambero 1 and Via Arenula 34 | www. tech-it-easy.it | bus 52, 53, 61, 71, 80, 85, 117*

MARKETS & FLEA MARKETS

MERCATINO FLAMINIO
(147 E2) *(𝄞 D5)*
Clothes, clothes, and more clothes, including vintage fashion. Popular flea market consisting of at least 240 stands

north of the Piazza del Popolo. *Sun 10am–7pm, closed in Aug | admission 1.60 euros Piazza della Marina 32 | tram 2, 19*

PORTA PORTESE ★
(151 D3–4) (*🕮 D11*)

You can find almost anything here – possibly including your stolen wallet, though of course it will be empty. Hats, shoes, binoculars, watches, out-of-the-ordinary clothing. And watch out for pickpockets! *Sun 7am–2pm | between Viale Trastevere and Porta Portese | bus H, 780 | tram 3, 8*

FASHION

ARMANI (145 E1) (*🕮 E7*)

His career plan was originally to become a surgeon, but then Giorgio Armani decided to operate in the world of fashion. His creations, whether a business outfit, the youthful Emporio line, perfumes or lifestyle products, are synonymous with Italian good taste. And the king of business fashion – noncrease, timeless, no wear and tear – still reigns at eighty plus with his flagship store close to the Spanish Steps. *Via Condotti 77 | www.armani.com | Metro A Spagna*

ARSENALE (144 B4) (*🕮 D8*)

Cutting-edge but not all that expensive. Designer fashion by Patrizia Pieroni. And you can also purchase one-off artworks here. *Via del Pellegrino 172 | www.patriziapieroni.it | bus 40, 62, 64*

CUCINELLI ★ (145 E1) (*🕮 E7*)

Brunello Cucinelli not only makes the very best cashmere hoodies, but the man from Umbria also has a reputation as a businessman with a social conscience. His factory is a former country estate in the enchanting village of Solomeo which he has completely restored. This style has rubbed off on his boutique in Via Borgognona. But you pay *prezzi alle stelle*, which is Italian for exorbitant! *Via Borgognona 33 | bus 52, 53, 61, 62, 80, 83*

EDO CITY (152 A1) (*🕮 G9*)

In Monti, fashion designer Alessandra Giannetti turns out suits for women, linen raincoats and casual trousers in select pastel colours in her very own Japanese-Italian style. *Via Leonina 78–79 | www.alessandragiannetti.com | Metro B Cavour*

FENDI (145 D1) (*🕮 E7*)

The five Fendi sisters rule over an empire of furs, fashion and cosmetics

TIME TO CHILL

If you would like to treat yourself after the rigours of sightseeing, here is an address that will do you good: in the ● *Centro Benessere* **(147 E3–4)** *(🕮 E6) (Via del Babuino 9 | tel. 06 32 88 88 20 | Metro A Flaminio | bus 117, 119, 490)* in the De Russie luxury hotel you can be pampered while hobnobbing with Rome's high society: sauna, gym, warm Jacuzzi with saltwater for approx. 45 euros, shiatsu massage and facials for around 75 euros. Book in advance! More indulgence for body and soul is on offer at the ● *Acanto Day Spa* **(145 D3)** *(🕮 E8) (Piazza Rondanini 30 | tel. 06 68 30 06 64 | www.acantospa.it | bus 70, 81, 87, 116, 492)*, where guests enjoy Asian tea, Thai massages and ethereal scents. From 70 euros.

The Via del Corso is also home to Rome's most exclusive shopping arcade: Galleria Alberto Sordi

(today belonging to the French luxury empire LVMH) with a showroom in a glass palazzo on the Corso. *Largo Carlo Goldoni 36–40 | www.fendi.com | Metro A Spagna*

FURLA (145 E1) *(ⓜ E7)*

In 1955 Aldo and Margherita sold their first leather bags for self-confident women. The upmarket bag producers from Bologna have opened a new store on Rome's most exclusive shopping street. *Via Condotti 55–56 | www.furla.com | bus 61, 62, 63 | Metro A Spagna*

LE GALLINELLE (152 B1) *(ⓜ G8)*

Imaginative ways of making something old into something new: in Monti, Wilma Silvestri recycles fabrics and transforms them into fantastic fashion – from ball gowns to summer bunting. *Via Panisperna 60 | Metro B Cavour*

GUCCI ★ (145 E1) *(ⓜ E7)*

World-famous and the ultimate in elegance: leather bags and exclusive fashion accessories by this luxury brand. *Via Condotti 8 | www.gucci.com | Metro A Spagna*

IBIZ ARTIGIANATO DI CUOIO ★ (144 C5) *(ⓜ D9)*

A chic, handmade leather clutch bag or garish purse? Since 1972, the Nepi family has made handcrafted leather goods and even for reasonable prices. You can glimpse how the new models are made in the back workshop. Loyal customers from around the world post Elisa Nepi selfies and proudly display their brand-new handbags. *Via dei Chiavari 39*

MASSIMO DUTTI (145 E2–3) *(ⓜ E8)*

The very best here is for men, the women's collection can't quite match it. *Via del Corso 14–16 | Galleria Alberto*

Bulgari sells jewellery, watches and accessories with a VIP cachet

Sordi | www.massimodutti.com | bus 62, 63, 116, 117, 119

MAX MARA (145 E1) (📖 E7)
Smart rags can be found at the Italian designer, who founded a fashion empire based on his parents' small dressmakers shop. *Via Condotti 17–19 and Via Frattina 28 | Metro A Spagna*

NUYORICA (144 C4) (📖 D9)
Stars like Cameron Diaz do their shopping here. The prices will make you gasp, but it's fun to look inside, and that's free. *Piazza Pollarola 36–37 | bus 40, 63, 116*

LA SELLA (139 E3–4) (📖 D8)
Fashionable leather bags, purses and wallets, belts, all at affordable prices. *Via della Cuccagna/Piazza Navona | bus 40, 46, 62, 64*

SERMONETA GLOVES ★
(145 E–F1) (📖 F7)
Leather gloves? Out of fashion for a long while, now they are a must-have again. Giorgio Sermoneta senior always believed in the return of elegance – and he now heads a glove emporium with stores in Milan, Venice and New York. His favourite shop is at the Spanish Steps in Rome. *Piazza di Spagna 61 | Metro A Spagna*

TALARICO (144 B3) (📖 D8)
This traditional Neapolitan tailor makes the top-end ties and cravats that Berlusconi and Bill Clinton wear. *Via dei Coronari 51 | bus 40, 62, 64*

TEMPI MODERNI (144 B4) (📖 D8)
Retro look: bracelets and necklaces in Sixties style, outlandish ties and hip bags. *Via del Governo Vecchio 108 | bus 62, 64a*

VALENTINO (145 E1) (📖 E7)
One of the last grand aristocrats of the fashion business, who helped to invent the dolce vita and at the age of over 80 still rules his empire. *Via Condotti 12–13 | Metro A Spagna*

OUTLET

CASTEL ROMANO OUTLET
(154 C6) (*∅ 0*)

Large discounts on luxury brands such as Trussardi, Ferré, Zegna, Loro Piano, Burberry, Lacoste or Calvin at the Castel Romano outlet on the Via Pontina approx. 25 km/15.5 mi to the south of the city centre. *Mon–Thu 10am–8pm, Fri–Sun 10am–9pm | Via Ponte di Piscina Cupa 64 | Castel Romano | 25 km/15.5 mi south of Rome | shuttle bus from Via Marsala 58 (Stazione Termini) | departures 9.30am, 9.55am, 11.30am, 12.30pm, 3pm, return 10.45am, 1.45pm, 5.15pm and 8.05pm | 13 euros | www.outlet-village.it/castelromano*

JEWELLERY

BIBELOT (144 A3) (*∅ C8*)

If you like small, pretty bric-a-brac and accessories, Art Nouveau jewellery and Gallé vases, then go to the sisters Valdete and Claudia for friendly advice and service. Also offers a jewellery repair service. *Via Banchi Nuovi 2 | bus 40, 62, 64*

BULGARI (137 E1) (*∅ E7*)

Perhaps you recognize the diamond-scaled reptile that is just swallowing a one-carat dazzler? The Serpenti bracelet is one of the icons made by the luxury jeweller. Sometimes, however, Bulgari also comes up with something nice: for example, the renovation and cleaning of the Spanish Steps (worth millions of euros) and the Barcaccia Fountain on Bulgari's doorstep. The window display is restrained, and the real treasure store is inside. *Via Condotti 10 | Metro A Spagna*

MELIS (136 C2) (*∅ C8*)

Goldsmith Massimo works with 21-carat gold for his regular customers, and produces modern items from 2000-year-old coins. *Via dell'Orso 57 | bus 116*

INSIDER TIP R-01-IOS
(145 D2) (*∅ M10*)

The name is not a secret code, but identifies the flagship store of Iosselliani, Rome's far-out pair of jewellery designers, Roberta and Paolo in Pigneto. Their other shop is in Tokyo-Shibuya. *Via del Pigneto 39a | www.iosselliani.com | tram 5, 19*

SHOES

BARRILÀ (147 E4) (*∅ E6*)

The name sounds like a spaghetti brand, but this is all about shoes. With flat pumps and ballerinas, you can cope with even the most uneven Roman cobblestones – and sandals in all colours of the rainbow are a hit, and quickly sold out. The small boutique is slightly too crammed full, but that shouldn't dissuade you! *Via del Babuino 33a | Metro A Spagna*

BORINI (136 C5) (*∅ D9*)

Shoes, almost too good to wear: this is a shoemaker for Rome's elegant circles. *Via dei Pettinari 86 | bus 23, 116 | tram 8*

TOD'S (137 D1) (*∅ E7*)

Diego della Valle is celebrated as the inventor of the gommini, elegant moccasins fitted with 133 nobs, with which he founded the famous brand Tod's. He made headlines as a patron of the arts by donating 25 million euros for restoring the crumbling Colosseum. *Via Fontanella Borghese 56/57 (Largo Goldoni) | bus 117*

ENTERTAINMENT

CITY **WHERE TO START?**
The trendy scene is alive and kicking in the **Pigneto** quarter. Around Via Pigneto **(153 E–F3)** *(⌂ M10)* there are more film clubs, book bars and creatively styled dance clubs than anywhere else. The downside is that Pigneto has fairly poor transport connections at night. As long as Metro C line is still under construction, you'll need a taxi back to the city centre.

Balmy evenings in the Roman open-air museum between the Vatican, Spanish Steps and Pantheon.

On warm evenings from April to October, Roman nightlife gets going in the small streets of the Centro Storico. Although there are numerous bars, cafés, wine bars and discos, the Romans prefer to stroll with friends until late at night in *corso* through the backstreets of the historic centre – past the magically illuminated ancient monuments and sparkling fountains that you can drink from. A stop for ice cream from one of the many popular *gelaterie* is also a must.

In addition to the centre and Trastevere, **INSIDER TIP** Monte Testaccio has also kept the charm of ancient Rome and is still a trendy meeting point. The same goes for the workers' and student quarter San Lorenzo, as well as Monti, Ostiense and Pigneto, which is situated on the roads heading out of the city Prenestina and Casilina.

Trastevere, Testaccio and the clubbing scene – but for young people in Rome, the real nightlife happens on the street

You can find out more about all events in the Thursday supplement "Trova Roma" of the daily newspaper "La Repubblica" or at *www.comune.roma.it, www.oggiroma.it* and *www.abcroma.com*.

BARS, CAFÉS & WINE BARS

Most clubs and discotheques have an admission charge in the shape of a membership pass (*tessera*) for approx. 15 euros, or otherwise 20–30 euros. Just occasionally the first drink is free.

BAR DEL FICO (144 B3) (*D8*)
Rustic, relaxed and authentic bar on a beautiful small Piazza, not too far from Piazza Navona. The ultimate meeting point for the trendy crowd. *Daily 8am–2am | Piazza del Fico 26 | bus 64, 71, 81, 492*

INSIDER TIP **BUM BUM DI MEL**
(144 B6) (*D10*)
Rome's coolest minibar: Mel, an attractive brazilian, mixes hot tropical cocktails in her tiny bar in the Trastevere. Young

Young Romans now hang out in Freni e Frizioni where cars were once repaired

Romans stand in queues for one of her drinks to then enjoy them out in the open. *Daily 6pm–1am | Via del Moro 17 | Tram 8 | bus H, 780*

CAFFÈ LATINO ⭐ (151 D5) (*D–E12*)
Buzzing location in the vaults of Monte Testaccio. *Tue–Sun | Via di Monte Testaccio 96 | tel. 0 65 78 24 11 | www.caffelatinodiroma.it | Metro B Piramide | bus 83, 121, 673*

CAVOUR 313 ⭐ (148 B6) (*G9*)
A hip wine bar with stylish people, tasty snacks and fresh salads. *Daily, closed Sun in summer | Via Cavour 313 | tel. 0 66 78 54 96 | www.cavour313.it | Metro B Via Cavour*

CUL DE SAC (144 C4) (*D8*)
Inside, the narrow, wood-panelled rooms are reminiscent of a cul-de-sac. This used to be a classic Roman wine and olive store. It still offers a fantastic array of *vini*, and you can choose from up to 1500 mainly Italian wines. Popular rendez-vous for young people. *Daily | Piazza Pasquino 73 | bus 40, 62, 64 | tram 8*

ENOTECA IL PICCOLO ● (144 B–C4) (*D8*)
Crowds of locals can be seen both in and outside this cafe-bar. Here you can hang out while watching the world go by. Enjoy a *caffè* during the day or an evening drink. Exclusive wine list, dry Prosecco, Aperol Spritz. *Daily noon–midnight | Via del Governo Vecchio 74 | bus 62, 64*

FONCLEA (144 A1) (*C7*)
A classic among the live music bars in the Prati. Jazz, rock, Dixie blues and funk every night. A move to the banks of the river under the Ponte Palatino (151 E2) (f E10) is done in summer *(Lungotevere degli Anguillara). Daily | Via Crescenzio 82 | www.fonclea.it | bus 34, 49, 87, 492*

INSIDER TIP ▶ FRENI E FRIZIONI
(144 B6) *(ω D10)*

Until recently this was a little car repair shop in Trastevere where *freni e frizioni* (brakes and clutches) were fixed. Now it's a popular bar. *Daily | Via del Politeama 4–6 | bus 23, 280, H | tram 8*

JONATHAN'S ANGELS (144 B3) *(ω D8)*
In this cult bar near Piazza Navona owner Jonathan has painted INSIDER TIP ▶ lavish frescoes on the walls – even in the toilets! *Tue–Sun | Via della Fossa 16 | bus 62, 64*

LEMONCOCCO (148 C2) *(ω H4)*
It's no trendy cocktail bar, but just an old-fashioned, green kiosk on the Piazza Buenos Aires. But for many Romans, Lemoncocco is about the flair of summer, sunshine and frivolity. Only one drink is available here: sweet coconut milk with freshly squeezed Sicilian lemon juice. The successful recipe is apparently 70 years old, Gian Luca, the friendly *barista* wouldn't reveal any more. A glass of *lemoncocco* costs 2 euros, with a shot (gin or vodka) 4 euros. *Daily 10.30am–2am | Piazza Buenos Aires | bus 63 | tram 3, 19*

OMBRE ROSSE ⭐
(151–152 C–D2) *(ω D10)*
The aperitif is also served with nibbles like *bruschetta, pizzette* or nuts. The pasta dishes like *spaghetti cacio e pepe* are simple, tasty and very reasonably priced. A pleasant square to linger and at the heart of the nightlife quarter, Trastevere. Extremely friendly service – almost a one-off in Rome. From September to April on Thursday evenings there is also live music (Jazz, Blues, Mardi Gras). *Mon–Sat 11am–2am | Piazza Sant'Egidio 12 | bus H, 23, 280 | tram 8*

RIVE GAUCHE 2 (149 F6) *(ω L8)*
A cross between a café, pub and disco in the San Lorenzo student quarter. The atmosphere is cosy; an excellent selction of craft beers. Happy hour till 9pm. *Daily | Via dei Sabelli 43 | tel. 0 64 45 67 22 | tram 3, 19 | bus 71, 30*

⭐ **Caffè Latino**
1968 atmosphere in Testaccio
→ **p. 94**

⭐ **Cavour 313**
A drink before bed in an authentic Italian osteria → **p. 94**

⭐ **Ombre Rosse**
Great for chillaxing in Trastevere, Thursdays with live music → **p. 95**

⭐ **Fanfulla 101**
This place throbs – an underground arts centre in Pigneto → **p. 96**

⭐ **Qube**
Mega-disco in spectacular surroundings in Tiburtino → **p. 96**

⭐ **Alexanderplatz**
Where the jazz stars jam – very close to the Vatican → **p. 97**

⭐ **Caruso Caffè**
Fiesta, salsa, Cuban son – sometimes live → **p. 97**

⭐ **Auditorium Parco della Musica**
Music mecca for international big names of all genres → **p. 98**

MARCO POLO HIGHLIGHTS

Men without a tie don't get in: the glamour-and-glitter disco Gilda

DANCE CLUBS

L'ALIBI (151 D5) (*D13*)
Rome's oldest-established gay disco with an enormous dance floor and roof terrace. You can have a film made of yourself dancing and download it at home. *Thu–Sat | Via di Monte Testaccio 44 | tel. 06 57 43 44 48 | Metro B Piramide | bus 23, 30*

BLACKOUT (0) (*M10*)
Just like the name says: black is what the teenagers here wear, and the music too is black. And there's also punk, rock, grunge and house. *Tue–Sat | Via Casilina 713 | tel. 06 24 15 04 7 | bus 105*

FANFULLA 101 ★ (0) (*M10*)
Pasolini, the Sixties film director with an unconventional lifestyle, would have loved this retro joint and underground arts centre in Pigneto, his favourite quarter. Live indie, jazz, rock, pop and art-house films. *Daily | Via Fanfulla da Lodi 101 | www.fanfulla.org | bus 81, 105, 810*

GILDA (145 E1) (*E–F7*)
Well-established fashionable club where politicians, B-list celebrities, well-heeled young business people and suburban *ragazzi* rub shoulders. *Thu–Sun, closed in summer | Via Mario dei Fiori 97 | www.gildabar.it | Metro A Spagna*

GOA (0) (*E15*)
Disco in Ostiense (near Università Roma 3) decked out in Bollywood style. A mix of oriental divan and club-lounge-restaurant. Funk and house. *Tue–Sun | Via Libetta 13 | tel. 06 57 48 27 77 | www.goaclub.com | Metro B Garbatella | bus 23*

QUBE ★ (0) (*0*)
A large-scale club in an old factory in Tiburtino, with a transgender programme: RadioRock on Thursdays, the gay show

Muccassassina on Fridays, *Babylon for all* on Saturdays. *Wed–Sat | Via di Portonaccio 212 | tel. 06 43 85 44 50 | www.qube disco.com | tram 5, 14, 19, get out at Prenestina/Via Portonaccio | bus 409*

RADIO LONDRA (151 D5) (𝄞 E13)

This themed bar named after an Allied radio station from the Second World War is absolutely in. The ambience is an improvised air-raid shelter with sandbags lying all around. The bar staff wear helmets. *Wed–Sun | admission 15 euros | Via di Monte Testaccio 67 | tel. 0 65 75 00 44 | www.radiolondradiscobar.com | Metro B Piramide | bus 23, 30*

ROOM 26 (0) (𝄞 0)

An ambitious project by a group of young art- and music enthusiasts at Piazza Marconi. It's all under one roof: from clubbing to disco, restaurant to modern art and photo exhibitions. *Thu–Sun | Piazza Marconi 31 | EUR District| www.room26.it | bus 170, 791*

JAZZ, FOLK & LATIN

ALEXANDERPLATZ ⭐
(146 B4) (𝄞 A–B6)

Italy's oldest jazz club where for more than 30 years almost all the greats have played is still swinging in Prati. Food and drinks remain something to be desired *Mon–Sat | admission 15 euros | Via Ostia 9 | tel. 06 39 72 18 67 | www.alexan derplatzjazzclub.com | Metro A Ottaviano–San Pietro | tram 19 | bus 492, 495*

CARUSO CAFFÈ ⭐
(151 D5) (𝄞 D13)

Fiesta, live bands, the hot tip for salsa, merengue, tango or Cuban son. Most Thursdays the band *Chirimia* plays. *Tue–Sun 11pm–4am | Via del Monte Testaccio 36 | tel. 0 65 74 50 19 | www.carusocafe. com | bus 95, 170, 781*

CASA DEL JAZZ (151 F5) (𝄞 F12)

A mafia boss once lived here. His confiscated villa with park is now a venue for jazz, jam sessions, festivals. *Viale di Porta Ardeatina 55 | tel. 06 70 47 31 | www.casajazz.it | Metro B Piramide | bus 30, 714*

CINEMAS & OPEN-AIR CINEMAS

AZZURRO SCIPIONI
(147 D3) (𝄞 C6)

Well-loved art-house cinema with film weeks devoted to avant-garde movies and international retrospectives from Robert Altman to Akira Kurosawa and Luchino Visconti. Some screenings with subtitles. *Via degli Scipioni 82 | tel. 06 39 73 71 61 | Metro A Lepanto*

LOW BUDGET

Free concerts are often held against a classical backdrop such as the Forum Romanum, Teatro Marcello, Pincio or Piazza Navona: for times see the Thursday supplement of "La Repubblica".

Roman *ragazzi* hang out till late at night on *Campo de' Fiori* **(144 C5) (𝄞 D9)**; when you meet outdoors, it costs nothing.

● Go to a club by the seaside for only 1.50 euros! In the evenings until 10.30pm a normal Metro or bus ticket will take you to the hip resort *Lido di Ostia* **(154 B6) (𝄞 0)** about 30 km/18.6 mi south of Rome, where you can hit the club scene. The first train back in the morning leaves at 5.18am.

INTRASTEVERE (144 B6) (*m D10*)

Film club in an alley near Piazza Trilussa in Trastevere, often screening films in the original English version. *Vicolo Moroni 3a | tel. 0 65 88 42 30 | bus H, 23 | tram 8*

NUOVO SACHER (151 D3) (*m D11*)

The production of cult director Nanni Moretti is called Sacher, and his own cinema is Nuovo Sacher – a declaration of his love for the cake of that name. INSIDER TIP In summer cinema under the stars. Sometimes discussions with the directors. *Largo Ascianghi 1 | tel. 0 65 818116 | www.sacherfilm.eu | tram 3, 8 | bus 75, 780*

THEATRE, OPERA, MUSICALS & CONCERTS

At last Rome can hold its head high vis-à-vis other great cities for classical music, theatre and opera thanks to the *Auditorium Parco della Musica*. You can also still hear good orchestras and choirs performing in the appropriate surroundings of a church, especially in the winter months. Baroque churches such as ● *Sant'Ignazio, Santa Maria del Popolo* and *Santa Maria in Aracoeli* form the stage for organ concerts and oratorios, with a wonderful atmosphere and for free. Sometimes the walls of the

Pantheon reverberate to the sound of Gregorian chants. For opera and concert listings, see *www.musicaroma.it*

AUDITORIUM PARCO DELLA MUSICA ★ (155 D4) (*m D2*)

A spectacular new concert centre that's not just immensely popular with Romans! During construction of this building designed by Renzo Piano the foundations of an ancient villa were discovered. They have been skilfully incorporat-

JAZZ IN A TRAM

● How retro is that? Rumble through Rome at night in a tram dating from 1947 while a jazz band plays or a few young opera singers belt out arias. The finishing touch is that the tram stops to let you dine with a view of the lit-up Colosseum. The food with fresh regional products and good wines is from the ◐ *Palatium* slow-food restaurant. *Mon–Sat 9pm from Porta Maggiore | Price 65 euros per person | Reservation essential, call mobile (Nunzia) 33 96 33 47 00 or www.tramjazz.com, www.listicket.it, www.romeguide.it*

Auditorium Parco della Musica: ultra-modern architecture for music by Renzo Piano

ed into the architecture. The Auditorium has three halls seating 2800, 1200 and 700 people which are connected by foyers and lead to an open-air amphitheatre. The complex includes a cafeteria, an exhibition about musical themes and a large shop for music and books, as well as a park with playground. *Park daily 11am–8pm | Viale Pietro de Coubertin 15 (near Stadio Flaminio) | tickets tel. 06 89 29 82 (*), from abroad tel. +39 02 60 06 09 00 | box office daily 11am–8pm | www.listicket.it | www. auditorium.com | tram 2, 19 | bus 53, 910*

TEATRO ARGENTINA (145 D4) *(𝓜 E8)*
The neo-Classical theatre on Largo Torre Argentina hosts performances by Italy's best ensembles, while young directors show what they can do at the avant-garde branch *Teatro India* (151 D5) *(𝓜 E9) (Via Luigi Pierantoni 6 | tram 8 | bus 170, H, 780 Piazza Radio)*, a former factory on the banks of the Tiber (near Stazione Trastevere). *Box office Tue–Sun 10am–2pm, 3–7pm | Largo di Torre Argentina 52 | tel. 0 66 84 00 03 45 | www.teatrodiroma.net | bus 62, 64*

TEATRO MARCELLO (145 D–E6) *(𝓜 E9)*
Concerts of chamber music, concerti del tempietto, are held after dark in the ancient amphitheatre. *Via del Teatro di Marcello 44 | tickets: www.classictic.com | bus 30, 63, 170*

TEATRO DELL'OPERA (148 B5) *(𝓜 G8)*
It may not be La Scala in Milan, but in 1990 the opera in the **INSIDER TIP** *Terme di Caracalla* (152 B4–5) *(𝓜 G12)*, which was otherwise known for its mediocrity, was made world-famous by the three tenors José Carreras, Plácido Domingo and Luciano Pavarotti. Following a long closure the impressive Baths of Caracalla have reopened, and in summer many performances are held there. *Box office Mon–Sat 10am–6pm, Sun 9am– 1.30pm | Piazza Beniamino Gigli 1 | tel. 06 48 16 01 | www.operaroma.it, www. listicket.it | Metro A Repubblica*

WHERE TO STAY

The Eternal City is a hugely popular destination. Twelve million visitors flock to Rome every year. During the Holy Year 2016, which Pope Francis rather spontaneously announced, apparently 20 million pilgrims and tourists arrived. Every sofa and spare room around Rome was full.

Whether you choose a stylish small B & B or luxury five-star hotel, or pilgrim accommodation or boutique hotel on a historic *palazzo* – in Rome, everybody finds suitable accommodation, from backpackers on a strict budget to pampered millionaires. Although the number of stars is not necessarily a guarantee of quality, in recent years hotel standards in Rome have markedly improved thanks to online feedback, Airbnb and the competition from Couchsurfing. Of course, there are always little surprises, like the whine of mopeds at night right outside your window or a disappointing hotel breakfast. If this happens to you, stay calm: in Rome it's different things that matter, for example the *grandezza* of the lobby with all its marble, plaster ceilings and perhaps a pretty courtyard. In some hotels a wonderful view from the top floor makes up for the dripping tap.

You'd like a double room for less than 100 euros as close as possible to St Peter's Square or the Colosseum? Forget it! It's not surprising that many people now focus on B & B or private accommodation where a double room costs between 70 and 150 euros. Alternatively, there are hostels from 25 euros,

Many hotels in Rome have a wonderful setting – but beware, as there is no guarantee they are quiet

with and without the enjoyment factor. When booking a hotel online, check whether the prices are inclusive of taxes, otherwise value added tax, possibly breakfast and a hotel tax of 2–3 euros will be added. From Easter until the end of October, it is high season with suitably high prices. Only August is less pricey, as then Italian tourists stay away: they all travel to the coast.

The historic city centre is closed to through traffic from 7am until 7pm and after 10pm, but as there are many res-idents in this area with their own vehi-cles, this is no guarantee that things will be quiet. If you have sensitive hearing, when you reserve ask for a quiet room *(una camera tranquilla)* looking out to the rear.

HOTELS: EXPENSIVE

BORGOGNONI (145 E2) *(∅ F7)*
Well-appointed hotel in a 17th-century palazzo that has kept its Baroque style. Close to Piazza S. Silvestro. *50 rooms |*

Rome's city hubbub stays outside: the courtyard of Donna Camilla Savelli

Via del Bufalo 126 | tel. 06 69 94 15 05 | www.hotelborgognoni.com | bus 53, 63, 492

CAPO D'AFRICA (152 B2) *(🕮 H10)*
Four-star hotel in a bright *palazzo* of the late 19th century, situated in a quiet street behind the Colosseum and the church of S. Clemente. Pleasant roof terrace for breakfast and sitting in the sun. *65 rooms | Via Capo d'Africa 54 | tel. 06 77 28 01 | www.hotelcapodafrica.com | Metro B Colosseo | tram 3 | bus 75, 85, 87*

DE RUSSIE (147 E3–4) *(🕮 E6)*
The five-star hotel at the foot of the Pincio, from the outside it looks like a modest 19th-century palazzo. It has an enchanting garden terrace with statues designed by Giuseppe Valadier, as well as Rome's best spa. *125 rooms and suites. Via del Babuino 9 | tel. 06 32 88 81 | www.hotelderussie.it | Metro A Flaminio | bus 490*

DONNA CAMILLA SAVELLI ★
(144 A6) *(🕮 C10)*
Rome lies at your feet! You stay overnight in a majestic villa designed by the Baroque master Borromini with painted beams and sloping stucco ceilings. Rooftop garden overlooking Rome and welcoming courtyard. *55 rooms | Via Garibaldi 27 | tel. 06 58 88 61 | www.hoteldonnacamillasavelli.com | bus 23, 280*

HOTEL ART ★ (147 F4) *(🕮 E6)*
Rome's coolest design hotel in a historic building lies in the peaceful artists' alley of Via Margutta near the Spanish Steps. The modern rooms are decorated in yellow, blue and orange. Lounge bar and gym. *47 rooms | Via Margutta 56 | tel. 06 32 87 11 | www.hotelart.it| Metro A Spagna*

HOTEL VICTORIA (148 B3–4) *(🕮 G6)*
A luxury hotel with Swiss flair: in the morning, you can jog in Villa Borghese park, which is situated opposite, and it's just a short five-minute walk to the Via Veneto. In the rooftop restaurant "Sopra i Pini" – a green oasis with palm trees, figs and a view of St Peter's – Rome's beautiful people meet for an aperitif or a business lunch to savour the summery and light Italian cuisine. Are

you an art lover? If the hotel owner Rolf Wirth has time, he will be glad to give you a tour of his unique gallery of Rome portraits in the hotel. Luxury for a reasonable price. *111 rooms | Via Campania 41 | tel. 06 42 37 01 | www.hotelvictoriaroma. com | bus 52, 53, 63, 80*

ROME CAVALIERI ☆ (154 C4) (*Ⅲ A3*)
Luxury hotel belonging to the Waldorf-Astoria group on Monte Mario with the exquisite La Pergola restaurant on the roof, a pool, tennis courts and a fine view over the city. *387 rooms and suites | Via Alberto Cadlolo 101 | tel. 0 63 50 91 | www. romecavalieri.it | bus 907, 913*

HOTELS: MODERATE

CASA VALDESE (147 D3) (*Ⅲ C–D6*)
Close to St Peter's, boasting a quiet location in the Prati quarter in a late 19th-century villa of the Waldensian church. Cosy atmosphere and ☆ **INSIDER TIP** lovely roof terrace. *33 rooms | Via Alessandro Farnese 18 | tel. 0 63 215 62 | www. casavalde seroma.it | Metro A Lepanto*

INSIDER TIP DOMUS AUSTRALIA
(148 C4) (*Ⅲ H6–7*)
Down under in Rome! The catholic archdiocese of Sydney, Australia, decided to convert the Roman accomodation for their pilgrims into a boutique hotel. Tasteful rooms, Aussie breakfast, cultural events and their own band. Close to Termini. *32 rooms | Via Cernaia 14b | tel. 0 64 88 87 81 | www.domusaustra lia.org | Metro B Repubblica | bus 60, 61, 62, 90*

FARNESE ☆ (147 D3) (*Ⅲ C6*)
You are in the heart of the city district of Prati, and the Pope lives nearby. An attractive old building with stylishly renovated interiors and surrounded by plenty of shops. Friendly service, and a good breakfast buffet, by local standards, with a ☆ view. *23 rooms | Via Alessandro Farnese 30 | tel. 0 63 21 25 53 | www. hotelfar nese.com | Metro A Lepanto*

MODIGLIANI ☆ (148 A5) (*Ⅲ F7*)
Excellent location near Via Veneto, quiet, tastefully furnished. See if you can book ☆ **INSIDER TIP** suite 602 with its rooftop view. Small courtyard garden. *24 rooms | Via della Purificazione 42 | tel. 06 42 81 52 26 | www.hotelmodiglia ni.com | Metro A Barberini | bus 52, 63*

NERVA ☆ (152 A1) (*Ⅲ F9*)
This charming, family-run hotel is ideally placed just behind Trajan's Forum

---

☆ **Donna Camilla Savelli**
Grand Baroque palace on the green Gianicolo hill → **p. 102**

☆ **Hotel Art**
Cool design and spacious rooms in an old palazzo → **p. 102**

☆ **Farnese**
Stay here to be close to the Vatican → **p. 103**

☆ **Modigliani**
Small and elegant near Via Veneto → **p. 103**

☆ **Nerva**
A romantic location behind Trajan's Forum → **p. 103**

☆ **Sant'Anselmo/Villa San Pio**
Stay in an Art Nouveau villa on the green Aventine Hill → **p. 104**

MARCO POLO HIGHLIGHTS

and is close to the Capitol, Coloseeum and popular nightlife of the Monti quarter. *19 rooms | Via Tor dei Conti 3 | tel. 0 66 78 18 35 | www.hotelnerva.com | Metro B Cavour | bus 75*

RAFFAELLO (148 C6) (*Ø G8*)

A small and elegant three-star hotel in the trendy Monti quarter. Quiet rooms with modern bathrooms and a good breakfast buffet, near Stazione Termini. *41 rooms | Via Urbana 3–5 | tel. 0 64 88 43 42 | www.hotelraffaello.it | Metro B Cavour | bus 117*

RICHMOND (152 A1) (*Ø F9*)

Small, pretty hotel between the Colosseum and Trajan's Forum. From the a terrace you get INSIDER TIP a wonderful view of the Foro Romano. Babysitters available. *13 rooms | Largo Corrado Ricci 36 | tel. 06 69 94 12 56 | www.hotelrichmondroma.com | Metro B Colosseo | bus 75, 87*

SANT'ANSELMO/VILLA SAN PIO ★

(151 E4) (*Ø E11*)

Do you crave some peace and the aromatic fragrance of oranges? Two quiet, well-kept Art Nouveau villas on the Aventine Hill with individually furnished rooms and nice gardens. *45 and 80 rooms | Piazza S. Anselmo 2 | Via di Santa Melania 19 | tel. 06 570 057 | www.aventinohotels.com | Metro B Circo Massimo*

SANTA MARIA

(150–151 C–D2) (*Ø D10*)

And at the heart of Transevere: a pretty three-star hotel in a former 16th-century monastery. You take breakfast by the orange trees in the courtyard. *18 rooms | Vicolo del Piede 2 | tel. 0 65 89 46 26 | www.htlsantamaria.com | tram 8 | bus H*

TEATRO DI POMPEO (144 C5) (*Ø D9*)

It's true, the entrance door is small and the lobby is unspectacular. But the rooms are comfortable – and you will sleep well

MORE THAN A GOOD NIGHT'S SLEEP

Have you already stayed the night in a monastery?
Solo donne, for women only, is the message at Orsa Maggiore Hostel **(150 C1)** **(*Ø C9*)** *(1 single from 60 euros, 2 double from 75 euros, 5 multi-bed rooms from 26 euros/person, discount in off-season | Via San Francesco di Sales 1a/ Via della Lungara | tel. 0 66 89 37 53 | www.orsamaggiorehostel.com)*, which is situated in a former convent – in the centre of Trastevere! The women's hostel is named in the *Casa delle Donne* after the "Great Bear" heavenly constellation, according to legend, a transformed nymph and nowadays a symbol

for "girl power". All the rooms are named after feminine star signs from Andromeda to Aphrodite.
Location, location, location – fantastic!
You're at the epicentre of everything here: in the mornings at Rome's most popular market, later for an aperitivo on the Piazza where the young Romans meet. The boutique hotel *Campo de' Fiori* **(144 C5)** **(*Ø D9*)** *(Via del Biscione 6 | tel. 06 68 80 68 65 | www.hotelcampodefiori.it | bus 40, 46, 62, 64, 116 | Expensive)* offers 23 small rooms with antiques and a 🌿 rooftop terrace with panoramic views. Nearby apartments also available (1–4 persons).

360°-panoramic view from the rooftop terrace and one of Rome's most beautiful Piazzas on the doorstep: Campo de' Fiori

above the walls of the ancient theatre, allegedly the place where Julius Caesar was murdered 2000 years ago. Campo de' Fiori, Piazza Navona, the Jewish Ghetto, all the spectacular attractions are nearby. *28 rooms | Largo Pallaro 8 | tel. 06 68 30 01 70 | www.hotelteatrodi pompeo.it | bus 40, 60, 64*

TRASTEVERE (151 D3) (*ጠ D10*)
Tiny refurbished hotel five minutes from Santa Maria in Trastevere with a view of the market, which will help you to wake up early. Mini-apartments for up to five people are available too. *9 rooms | Via Luciana Manara 24 | tel. 06 58 14 713 | www.hoteltrastevere.net | tram 8 | bus H*

LA ZOTTA (144 A5) (*ጠ C9*)
Elegant bed & breakfast in a small 17th century palazzo on the edge of Traste-vere. The architect couple from Rome

rents two quiet rooms and a suite (1–4 pers.). *3 rooms | Via San Francesco di Sa-les 88/Int. 4 | tel. 06 68 30 88 93 | mobile tel. 33 56 62 93 24 | www.lazotta.it | bus 23*

HOTELS: BUDGET

ANTICO BORGO (151 D3) (*ጠ D10*)
Tiny hotel in a little alley in Trastevere. The rooms are relatively small and not very bright, but the location is superb, and it's fairly quiet for Trastevere. Break-fast is served in the rooms. *11 rooms | Vicolo del Buco 7 | near Piazza del Drago | tel. 06 58 83 77 74 | tram 8 | bus H*

APOLLO (152 A1) (*ጠ G9*)
Small, good-quality, and a great loca-tion in trendy Monti, less than five min-utes from the Colosseum and Forum Ro-manum. A good breakfast is served in the pretty ☼ roof garden with a view

of the city centre. 24 rooms | *Via dei Serpenti 109* | *tel. 0 64 88 58 89* | *www.hotelapollorome.com* | *Metro B Cavour* | *bus 40, 60, 64, 117*

AZZURRA (148 A5) (*Ⓜ F7*)

No great luxury, but a first-class location near the Fontana di Trevi and helpful staff. *8 rooms* | *Via del Boccaccio 25* | *tel. 0 64 74 65 31* | *www.hotelazzurra.com* | *Metro A Barberini* | *bus 52, 53, 60, 61, 62, 492*

EDERA (152 B–C2) (*Ⓜ H10*)

Elegant little Art Nouveau hotel between the Colosseum and Piazza Vittorio Emanuele. The rooms have been refurbished, and some of them are furnished with antiques. You can reach the Lateran on foot or by tram. Small garden. *28 rooms* | *Via Angelo Poliziano 75* | *tel. 06 70 45 38 88* | *www.hotelederaroma.com* | *tram 3*

GRIFO (152 A1) (*Ⓜ G9*)

Basic guesthouse with three- and four-bed rooms as well as doubles, offering breakfast on the roof terrace in the romantic Monti quarter. *19 rooms* | *Via del Boschetto 144* | *tel. 0 64 87 13 95* | *www.hotelgrifo.com* | *Metro B Cavour* | *bus 64, 117*

IVANHOE (152 B1) (*Ⓜ G9*)

Reasonably priced little hotel at the heart of Monti with all its pubs and down-to-earth atmosphere. The Colosseum and Forum Romanum, Santa Maria Maggiore and the Termini station are within walking distance. Small rooms, roof terrace. *26 rooms* | *Via Urbana 92a* | *tel. 06 48 68 13* | *www.hotelivanhoe.it* | *Metro B Cavour* | *bus 71, 117*

KATTY (149 D5) (*Ⓜ J7*)

Katty is almost an institution close to Termini railway station. Quite a few guests remember staying here in the 1980s when the formidable mamma was here. Now, the daughter is the manager with her abrupt, Roman charm. A wonderful old-fashioned lift brings you and your luggage to the 5th floor. Here, the rooms are spacious, clean and relatively quiet. Breakfast is in true Roman style at the bar on the corner. *18 rooms* | *Via Palestro 35* | *tel. 0 64 44 12 16* | *www.hotelkatty.it* | *bus 492*

KRISTI (148 C4) (*Ⓜ H6*)

Pleasant, modest guesthouse for young people, tiny rooms but well-situated near the HQ of the (unpopular) tax authorities and the (popular) state president in the Quirinal Palace. *10 rooms* | *Via*

LOW BUDGET

Affordable apartments and studios are on offer at *www.friendlyrentals.com/Rome* and *www.only-apartments.com/Rome.* Bargains like a 4-room flat for 6 people at 180 euros near the Vatican Museums, however, are booked out before you can say a Hail Mary.

A popular address for young people is *Village Flaminio* **(155 D3)** *(Ⓜ O)* *(Bungalow sleeping 5 from 132 euros* | *Via Flaminia Nuova 821* | *tel. 0 63 33 26 04, 063 33 14 29* | *www.villageflaminio.com* | *local train towards Prima Porta from Piazzale Flaminio, the stop is Due Ponti* | *by car: from GRA Gran Raccordo Annulare uscita (exit) 6 in the direction of Flaminio/Roma Centro, as far as Corso Francia)* in the north of Rome, a campsite in green surroundings with a pool.

Its style is almost fashionable again, and the location is fantastic: Hotel Mimosa

Collina 24 | tel. 06 47 44 90 02 | www.rome hotelkristi.it | Metro A Repubblica | bus 60, 62, 63, 90, 492

LOCANDA CARMEL (150 C3) (∅ C10)
Basic rooms and a wonderful roof garden in Trastevere. 11 rooms | Via Goffredo Mameli 11 | tel. 06 58 09 99 21 | www.hotel carmel.it | rram 8 | bus H, 75, 780

MIMOSA (145 D4) (∅ E8)
Right by the Pantheon! The furniture is a bit worn but the staff are cheerful. 11 rooms | Via di Santa Chiara 61 | tel. 06 68 80 17 53 | www.hotelmimosa.net | bus 64, 116

INSIDERTIP PARADISE (146 C3) (∅ B4)
Owner Luigi is straight-up and easy to deal with. There's no breakfast but a fair discount for young couples who are happy to be cosy in the 1.20 m bed in the single room. There are doubles, also three- and four-bed rooms. 10 rooms | Via Giulio Cesare 47 | tel. 06 36 00 43 31 | www.

pensioneparadise.com | Metro A Lepanto | tram 19 | bus 70, 590, 913

BED & BREAKFAST

In recent years more and more bed & breakfasts have opened up in Rome, organised through agencies like the Bed and Breakfast Association of Rome (tel. 06 55 30 22 48 | www.b-b.rm.it); Tomas b&b (Viale Giulio Cesare 183 | tel. 06 66 53 58 55 | www.tomasbbrome.com | Metro A Ottaviano) lets five rooms (80–100 euros) near the Vatican; Anne & Mary (Via Cavour 325 | tel. 06 69 94 187 | www.anne-mary.com) offer three well-kept rooms (100–150 euros) close to the Colosseum. Natalia Bianchi (mobile tel. 033 92 14 20 09 | dolce_roma.@yahoo.it) has two flats near the Colosseum.

The following are also worth a look: www.caffelletto.it, accommodation in high-class houses. For further addresses: www.bb-roma.it | tel. 06 68 13 56 77, and www.bedandbreakfastroma.com.

If you want to stay in Trastevere, book early

For environmentalists there's the ☯ *Bed & Breakfast Bio (3 rooms | Via Cavalese 28 | mobile tel. 32 86 21 94 84 | 33 57 15 17 49 | www.bedandbreakfast bio.com)* in Monte Mario district. Organic breakfast will be served on the terrace.

MONASTERIES

Roman Catholic pilgrims who require cheap accommodation should apply to the local archdiocese in their home country. The accommodation pages of *www. romeguide.it* include a list of religious institutions.

CASA DI PROCURA DELL'ORDINE TEUTONICO (149 F1) (𝄜 M2)

A guesthouse with a palm garden. With the nuns of the Teutonic Order in Nomentano, north of the centre with a direct bus connection to Piazza Venezia, you are in good hands. *26 rooms | Via Nomentana 421 | tel. 06 86 21 80 12 | www.gaeste haus-rom.it | bus 36, 60, 82, 90*

ISTITUTO MARIA SS. BAMBINA (146 B5) (𝄜 B8)

Nowhere is closer to the Pope! The accommodation run by nuns right on St Peter's Square is greatly sought-after by pilgrims, as you can almost look into the Pope's study. So book well ahead (room from 50 euros). *35 rooms | Via Paolo VI 21 | tel. 06 69 89 35 11 | www.suoredimari abambina.org | bus 46, 64, 571, 916*

ISTITUTO PADRI TEATINI (144 C4) (𝄜 D9)

A good address specially for youthful pilgrims. Behind Sant'Andrea della Valle. *120 beds | Piazza Vidoni 6 | tel. 06 68 61 33 9 | www.teatino.com/ ostello | bus 62*

SUORE IMMACOLATE (145 F1) (𝄜 F7)

Convent of the "Sisters of the Immaculate Conception" near the Spanish Steps, with nine rooms. *Via Sistina 113 | tel. 06 47 45 32 4 | Metro A Spagna*

HOSTELS

In Rome, hostels also offer an alternative, since with prices starting at 18 euros per person in a dorm they are unbeatable value for young people who don't expect high standards but want to stay somewhere central. Furthermore you can meet people from all over the world. Bookings through e.g. *www.hostelworld.com*, *www.hostelbookers.com* or enquire in person at the addresses below.

ALESSANDRO PALACE HOSTEL
(149 D5) (*Ш J7*)

Palazzo or hostel? In any case, this is a fabulous spot for relaxing at the heart of the student quarter San Lorenzo, seven minutes on foot to Termini railway station, where the airport buses also depart. In-house bar, free WiFi and ☆ rooftop garden. *8 rooms | Via Vicenza 42 | tel. 06 44 61 95 8 | www.hostelalessandro.com | bus 38 | tram 3, 19 | Metro B Castro Pretorio | Metro A/B Termini*

CIAK HOSTEL (152 C2) (*Ш J10*)
Cheap hostel near the Colosseo. *Viale Manzoni 55 | tel. 06 77 07 67 03 | www.ciakhostel.com | Metro A Manzoni*

LA CONTRORA (148 B4) (*Ш G7*)
Popular accomodation from 26 euros between Termini and Villa Borghese. *Via Umbria 7 | tel. 0 69 83 73 66 | www.hostelsclub.com | Metro A Barberini*

PENSIONE OTTAVIANO HOSTEL
(146 B4) (*Ш B6*)

Rome's oldest hostel has seen generations of backpackers: here they can dump their packs right by the Vatican. *Via Ottaviano 6 | tel. 06 39 73 81 38 | www.pensioneottaviano.com | Metro A Ottaviano*

FOR BOOKWORMS AND FILM BUFFS

Imperium – An unknown young lawyer, highly intelligent, a good speaker, sensitive and hugely ambitious enters the halls of power. In Washington D. C.? No, in Rome! Robert Harris' historical thriller is set over 2000 years ago, and the lawyer with ambitions to reach the top is called Marcus Tullius Cicero. The author of "Pompeii" and "The Ghost" again shows how cool history can be (2006).

La Grande Bellezza – Rome was rarely depicted so wonderfully and so decadently, and back in 2014 Paolo Sorrentino won an Oscar and a Golden Globe for his work. Sorrentino's main character, journalist Jep Gambardella, has written a unique and amazing novel. Since then he is swinging through Roman high society – not so much wild parties any longer, beautiful yet not so young women and enigmatic, resigned characters. On his 65th birthday Gambardella is seized by existential boredom. A film with grandiose images. *Complimenti!*

To Rome with Love – After London, Barcelona and Paris, it was just Rome's turn! Woody Allen filmed a turbulent romantic comedy for the n-th time; this time the old master cleverly mixes his stars like Jesse Eisenberg, Ellen Page and Alec Baldwin with an appearance by his director colleague Roberto Benigni and his own stunt: a homage to Rome and its great filmmaker, Federico Fellini (2012)

DISCOVERY TOURS

① ROME AT A GLANCE

START: ① Colosseo
END: ⑬ Teatro Marcello

1 day
Walking/driving time
(without stops)
3 hours

Distance:
➡ 6 km/3.7 mi

COSTS: 1-day bus/Metro ticket 6 euros
Lift at ⑤ Monumento Nazionale a Vittorio Emanuele II 7 euros
Combined ticket for the ② Foro Romano and ① Colosseo 12 euros
WHAT TO PACK: water, sun protection

IMPORTANT TIPS: To avoid the queues for the ① Colosseo remember
to buy the combined admission ticket for the Foro Romano/Colosseo
at the new forum entrance, by the Colosseum at the Arco di
Constantino, or ideally online beforehand. ⑦ San Pietro is closed on
Wednesday mornings due to the audience with the Pope.

Would you like to explore the places that are unique to this city? Then the Discovery Tours are just the thing for you – they include terrific tips for stops worth making, breathtaking places to visit, selected restaurants and fun activities. It's even easier with the Touring App: download the tour with map and route to your smartphone using the QR Code on pages 2/3 or from the website address in the footer below – and you'll never get lost again even when you're offline.

→ p. 2/3

Rom is unique, magnificent and has been a cult destination for almost 3000 years. Take a personal tour of this amazing city with a cappuccino over the Capitol, a stroll through its ancient history, a visit to St. Peter's, *aperitivo* on the piazza and evening meal in the ghetto.

09:00pm Slept well? Camera at the ready? Then start the day at the **❶ Colosseo** → p. 30. Have you already bought the combination ticket Forum/Colosseo online? Then you can now visit the magnificent ancient monuments almost without waiting in queues. **At the entrance near the Arch**

❶ Colosseo 🏛

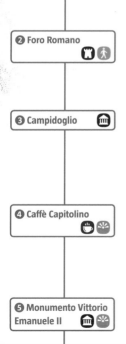

② Foro Romano 🏛️🚶

③ Campidoglio 🏛️

④ Caffè Capitolino ☕🍽️

⑤ Monumento Vittorio Emanuele II 🏛️🍽️

of Constantine, legionnaires are often standing in historical costume and ready to pose for a photo. But be careful – the "fees" are totally exorbitant! Carry on to other ancient sites, because **very close by is the ② Foro Romano → p. 35**. Enjoy the walk **over the Via Sacra** to the centre of power in ancient Rome. **At the Arco di Settimo Severo head left and make climb up to the new exit of the Forum below the Capitol.**

`12:00pm` You have now reached the **③ Campidoglio → p. 29**, the heart of Rome, with the **Piazza del Campidoglio** designed by Michelangelo. On the oval Piazza is a copy of the statue of Emperor Marcus Aurelius. The original one stands majestically in the Musei Capitolini → p. 36 – you should save a visit here for another day. Do you feel like a coffee? Then, try a cappuccino in the **④ Caffè Capitolino** (Tue–Sun 9.30am–7pm | Piazzale Caffarelli 4) above the museum, which also has a fabulous rooftop terrace. You will need your museum ticket, **simply walk to the right around the Palazzo to the side entrance, and then climb the steps to the terrace.** Do you want to climb higher for an even more sensational view of the Eternal City? Then from Piazza Venezia take the entrance into the snow-white **⑤ Monumento Vittorio Emanuele II → p. 36**. On the right-hand side and slightly hidden, you will find a glass lift (7 euros) that transports you high up to the Quadriga where the domes, churches and Palazzi of Rome lie at your feet.

01:00pm Has ancient Rome given you an appetite? Then treat yourself in the ❻ **Terre e Domus Enoteca** *(Mon–Sat 7.30am–midnight | Foro Traiano 82/Via dei Fori Imperiali | Budget–Moderate)* to hearty regional cuisine from Latium Province. This is the only good restaurant near the Forums, so at lunchtime it is crowded. The wines are also excellent here, but you have a full itinerary. St Peter is waiting! **From Piazza Venezia (bus stop Via del Plebiscito) take bus 64 in the direction of the Stazione San Pietro and hop off at the bus stop Cavalleggeri/San Pietro.**

03:00pm Now you are standing in front of ❼ **San Pietro → p. 61**, one of Christendom's most imposing churches. In front of it, on the **Piazza San Pietro → p. 61** designed by Bernini with its elegant ellipse-shaped colonnades, throngs of Catholics assemble every Wednesday for an audience with the Pope. **On the right-hand colonnades you'll see the security checks to St Peter's Basilica.** In the Musei Vaticani → p. 56 with the Cappella Sistina → p. 58 you would arrive from the right of the Vatican ensemble, but you should plan an extra day for this – the art treasures here simply play havoc with any timetable. To reach ❽ **Castel Sant'Angelo → p. 54** with its splendid view over the city, **walk along the Via della Conciliazione.** Inspired by Bernini's elegant statues of angels – and pestered by all the street sellers – take the **Ponte Sant'Angelo back into the Centro Storico. From the Via del Spirito Santo, head along the** ❾ **Via dei Banchi Nuovi**, a pretty street with small jewellery shops such as **Bibelot → p. 91,** gold-leaf frame makers, second-hand shops, cafes and trattorias. **Follow the also lively Via del Governo Vecchio to Il Pasquino**, one of the famous talking statues, the Statue parlanti → p. 126. From there, it is just a few steps to the magnificent ❿ **Piazza Navona → p. 45**. If you are wilting by this stage, a gelato, for example an organic ice cream at **Grom → p. 73**, or *caffè* enjoyed among a colourful crowd of people will liven you up again.

07:00pm To finish your day, **stroll along the Via della Cuccagna and the Via dei Baullari to** ⓫ **Campo de' Fiori → p. 41**, where you can order an *aperitivo* and linger in wonderful surroundings until evening as this is the

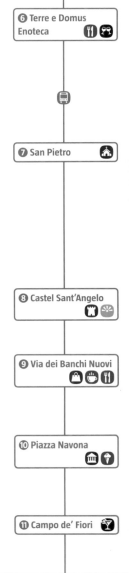

❻ Terre e Domus Enoteca 🍴 ✄

🚌

❼ San Pietro 🏠

❽ Castel Sant'Angelo 🎭 🧭

❾ Via dei Banchi Nuovi 💍 ☕ 🍴

❿ Piazza Navona 🏛 🍦

⓫ Campo de' Fiori 🍽

rendezvous for the Roman *ragazzi*. By 8pm the many trattorias of the district will be filling up. **Go along the Via dei Giubbonari** and on both sides of the Via Arenula you'll enter the picturesque ghetto with its revived Roman-Jewish scene. **From the Via dei Falegnami, take a detour to the** Fontana delle Tartarughe → p. 43 on the Piazza Mattei. **Back on the Via Portico d'Ottavia** try some Roman and Jewish specialities at  **Ristorante Il Giardino Romano** *(Thu–Tue noon–11pm | Via del Portico d'Ottavia 18 | tel. 06 68 80 96 61 | Moderate)*. After a good meal, stroll through the **Portico d'Ottavia**, which Emperor Augustus had built for his sister Ottavia in 27 AD, to the illuminated ⓲ **Teatro Marcello** → p. 44, where classical concerts are held in summer.

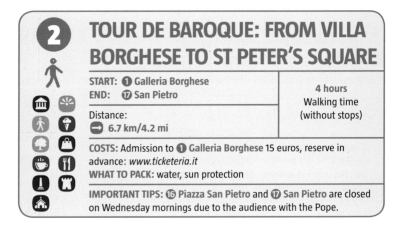

2 TOUR DE BAROQUE: FROM VILLA BORGHESE TO ST PETER'S SQUARE

START: ① Galleria Borghese END: ⓱ San Pietro	4 hours Walking time (without stops)
Distance: 🔜 6.7 km/4.2 mi	

COSTS: Admission to ① Galleria Borghese 15 euros, reserve in advance: *www.ticketeria.it*
WHAT TO PACK: water, sun protection

IMPORTANT TIPS: ⓰ Piazza San Pietro and ⓱ San Pietro are closed on Wednesday mornings due to the audience with the Pope.

Without them the Rome we know would not exist! The star architects of Baroque Gianlorenzo Bernini and Francesco Borromini were bitter rivals – but between the two of them they turned Rome into a magnificent Baroque stage. The melancholic Borromini intrigued against the charismatic Bernini, who served eight popes over a 60-year career and found that fame, wealth and women fell into his lap. Follow both of these geniuses on this Tour de Baroque.

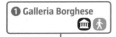

10:00am Start your tour at the ① **Galleria Borghese** →p. 50 *(don't forget you have to book tickets in advance!)*, the best place for getting an impression of Bernini's early works as a sculptor, from the somewhat clumsy-looking "David" to the radiant nakedness of "Apollo and Daph-

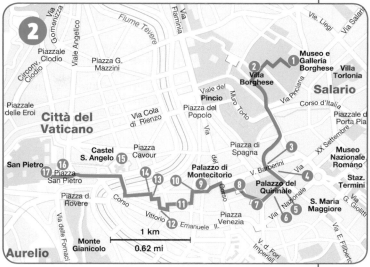

ne". **Stroll through the gardens of the ❷ Villa Borghese** → p. 54 and enjoy a cappuccino in the **Cinecaffè** *(daily 9am–9pm | Largo Marcello Mastroianni 1 | Budget–Moderate)*, before you head **along the Via Veneto**, the street for exclusive cafés, hotels and the dolce vita, to ❸ **Piazza Barberini**, where Bernini left his mark twice: At the corner of Via Veneto and Via Basilio splashes the "bee fountain", the **Fontana delle Api**. Three bees were the heraldic symbol of the Barberini pope family. On the piazza Bernini's elegant **Fontana del Tritone** with its sensuous Neptune seems to spread a feeling of lightness of being.

When you turn **into the steep Via Quattro Fontane**, you'll notice on your left the three-storey façade of the ❹ **Palazzo Barberini**, which was started by Borromini but was finished by his arch-rival Bernini with his triumphant synthesis of several columns. Today this palace is the **Galleria Nazionale d'Arte Antica a Palazzo Barberini** *(Tue–Sun 8.30am–7pm | admission 7 euros)*. **At the crossing with four fountains, turn into the long Via Quirinale**, where you can see another example of the poisoned but creative rivalry between the two architects. In the little church ❺ **San Carlo** → p. 52, often nicknamed by the Romans as San Carlino, Borromini, with sparing use of materials, achieved a graceful but austerely composed oval interior that creates an illusion of height.

❷ Villa Borghese

❸ Piazza Barberini

❹ Palazzo Barberini

❺ San Carlo

⑥ Sant'Andrea al Quirinale

⑦ Piazza del Quirinale

⑧ Fontana di Trevi

⑨ Palazzo Montecitorio

⑩ Gelateria Giolitti

⑪ Piazza Sant'Eustachio

⑫ Piazza Navona

His colleague Bernini – as usual – was anything but sparing in his means. The two-storey wedding church of **⑥ Sant'Andrea al Quirinale** → p. 52 **less than 200 m/ 656 ft away,** also oval but with the longer axis set laterally, has an impressive, monumental entrance and steps. Beyond it is the massive, conspicuous INSIDER TIP **Fontana dei Dioscuri**, from Antiquity, on which the colossal statues of the Dioscuri Castor and Pollux, taken from the Baths of Constantine, hold on to an obelisk that Emperor Augustus brought back from Egypt as a souvenir.

From the **⑦ Piazza del Quirinale** you can enjoy a vast panorama of the city before **passing the Palazzo del Quirinale to descend the low steps of the Via Dataria.** Soon you will hear the splashing of the **⑧ Fontana di Trevi** → p. 49 Rome's most sensuous fountain was built by Nicolas Salvi, but did you know that the designs were drawn up by a certain Gianlorenzo Bernini? **Now stroll across the Piazza Colonna with its column of Marcus Aurelius** – and you are now in the political arena of modern Italy. Pass the **Palazzo Chigi**, the seat of government, and continue to **⑨ Palazzo Montecitorio**, adorned with obelisks and a curving façade designed by Bernini in 1655, and which appears every evening on the Italian TV news as it is the seat of the national parliament. Time for ice cream? **Take a slight detour over the Piazza Montecitorio to the Via Uffici del Vicario** directly to the **⑩ Gelateria Giolitti** → p. 73, Rome's oldest ice-cream shop.

By way of the Pantheon → p. 45 you come to the small and intimate **⑪ Piazza Sant'Eustachio**, with its namesake **bar**, which is said to have the best coffee in Rome. Continue on to the **Corso Rinascimento** from where you can enjoy a view of Borromini's bizarre masterpiece **Sant'Ivo alla Sapienza** The church with a Baroque façade oscillating between convex and concave curves has the ground plan of a bee. The architect hoped to flatter his immodest patron, Urban VIII, with this reference to the heraldry of the Barberini family. **After crossing Corso Rinascimento you reach ⑫ Piazza Navona** → p. 45, the centrepiece of which is Bernini's **Fontana dei Quattro Fiumi**. The church of **Sant'Agnese** is – you guessed it – by his enemy Borromini. **Leave the Piazza along the Via Tor Milina and walk past a former artistic highlight, the church** Santa Maria della Pace → p. 46 with Raphael's

Justin Timberlake, Cameron Diaz and the Obama family have all visited the Gelateria Giolitti

frescoes of the Sibyls. In the **⓭ Caffetteria Chiostro del Bramante → p. 72** next door, you can browse through art books in the bookshop, visit the exhibitions or simply enjoy some refreshment.

`01:00pm` **Next take the Via dei Coronari,** the street of antique dealers, **on your way to the Tiber.** Time for lunch? How about a pranzo at the **⓮ Osteria dell'Antiquariato** *(daily | Piazzetta di San Simeone 26 | tel. 0 66 87 96 94 | Moderate)* on the pretty **Piazzetta di San Simeone?** Your route then takes you **over the Ponte Sant' Angelo,** completed in 136 AD by Emperor Hadrian to give access to his mausoleum, on top of which the papal fortification **⓯ Castel Sant'Angelo → p. 54** stands. It was Bernini who turned it into Rome's most graceful bridge by adding serene statues of angels to whom he lent sensuous folds of drapery and a coquettish smile that is more of this world than the next. The last stop on your walk is the apotheosis, Bernini's boldest work with Christian intention: the ellipse-shaped **⓰ Piazza San Pietro → p. 61,** which seems to embrace all of Christendom with open arms.

⓭ Caffetteria Chiostro del Bramante

⓮ Osteria dell'Antiquariato

⓯ Castel Sant'Angelo

⓰ Piazza San Pietro

⑰ San Pietro 🏠

You end your tour in **⑰ San Pietro → p. 61** standing under Bernini's bronze baldachin, a structure for which both artists should be given credit. Its famous volutes were in fact designed by Borromini yet in those days the term copyright had not yet been invented: Bernini paid Borromini just a tenth of his wage for his work and threw him out shortly before the baldachin was completed.

③ GREEN ROME: TRASTEVERE, GIANICOLO AND THE TIBER

START: ① Piazza Sonnino
END: ① Piazza Sonnino

Distance:
📍 5 km/3.1 mi

4 hours
Walking time
(without stops)
1.5 hours

COSTS: Bus ticket to the ① Piazza Sonnino 1,50 euros
WHAT TO PACK: water, sun protection

When you have visited so many museums and ancient forums that your head is reeling, your feet are tired from all of the ancient city's cobbled streets and you yearn for nature and a view further afield, then look for some relaxation on the 84 m (275 ft)-high Gianicolo hill which is dedicated to the Roman Janus.

① Piazza Sonnino 🚶

② Piazza Santa Maria in Trastevere 🏠

③ Caffè di Marzio ☕

④ Tempietto 🏛

⑤ Fontana dell'Acqua Paola 🏛

`10:00am` Start your walk at the **① Piazza Sonnino**. in Trastevere, an old artisan's quarter. Stroll **along the Via della Lungaretta** until you reach **② Piazza Santa Maria in Trastevere**, named after the oldest church in Rome that is dedicated to the **Virgin Mary → p. 65**. The golden mosaic over the narthex sparkles as you approach. Did you miss out on breakfast today? Popular with Romans, the **③ Caffè di Marzio** (Thu–Mon 8am–2pm, Tue 10am–10pm | Budget–Moderate) offers small snacks, fresh juices and cappuccino. **Follow the Via della Paglia and then Via Garibaldi** to the church San Pietro in Montorio. With a diameter of just 5.50 m/18 ft, the **④ INSIDER TIP Tempietto** by Bramante in the courtyard of the adjoining Franciscan monastery is a miniature masterpiece of High Renaissance architecture.

Continue on the Via Garibaldi taking the shortcut via the steps of San Pancrazio until you hear the rushing water in the **⑤ Fontana dell'Acqua Paola.** In 1612, Pope Paul V commissioned Carlo Maderno to build these pompous

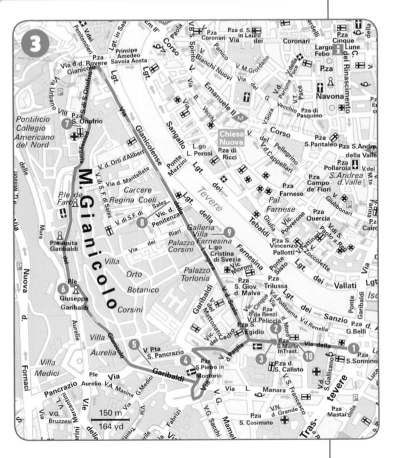

fountains which were supplied with water from the restored aqueduct from imperial times. **On the Passeggiata del Gianicolo surrounded by green space, head up the hill.**

12:00pm Try to reach the ⑥ **Piazza Garibaldi** by noon. Here a cannon salute is fired as in olden days at exactly 12 o'clock. From the square with the striking equestrian statue of Giuseppe Garibaldi (1807–82), a hero of Italian liberation, the view is stunning. **Follow the path** through the gardens to a woman seated on her horse, a pistol in her hand and holding her son in her arms. There are cavaliers cast in bronze all over the world, but it's not often you see a INSIDERTIP statue of a female rider: this is

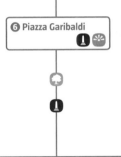

⑥ Piazza Garibaldi

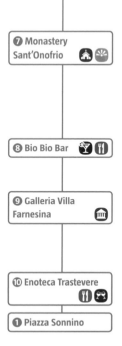

Anita Garibaldi Ribeiro, a Brazilian woman who travelled with her husband from one country to another, bore his children and lost them – all in the name of freedom for South America. Enjoy the splendid view in th **❼ Monastery Sant'Onofrio** including the Baroque frescoes in the monastery's courtyard. Now **descend the Salita S. Onofrio to Piazza della Rovere**, where the Tiber and traffic await you.

❼ Monastery Sant'Onofrio

01:00pm Turn right **at the Palazzo Salviati into the Via della Lungara** along the Tiber. In the former courtyard of a monastery, you'll find the ❽ **Bio Bio Bar** *(Tue–Fri 9am–8pm)*. Time for an *aperitivo* or a simple vegetarian meal. The bar belongs to the Casa Internazionale delle Donne. **Then follow the Via della Lungara** until you reach the **❾ Galleria Villa Farnesina** → S. 55. In the small yet exquisite Renaissance palace, take time to marvel at Raphael's frescoes "Cupid and Psyche" where the mistress of the palace owner is supposed to have modelled for the painter. To complete your tour, **stroll along the Via della Scala to the old Trastevere.** If you've only had time for a drink until now, enjoy a fresh salad, *bruschetta* or a plate of pasta in the lively ❿ **Enoteca Trastevere** *(daily noon–1am | Via della Lungaretta 86 | Moderate)* before you return to the ❶ **Piazza Sonnino**.

❽ Bio Bio Bar

❾ Galleria Villa Farnesina

❿ Enoteca Trastevere

❶ Piazza Sonnino

Catholic mass in the Domitilla Catacombs on the Via Appia Antica

4 ANCIENT ROME BY BICYCLE ON THE VIA APPIA ANTICA

START: ❶ Information office Via Appia Antica	**4 hours**
ZIEL: ⓬ Villa dei Quintili	Cycling time
Distance:	(without stops)
➡ 9 km/5.6 mi	1.5 hours

COSTS: Hire a bike for 15 euros a day, bus ticket 1.50 euros a ride, admission to the separate Catacombs 8 euros each
WHAT TO PACK: water, sun protection

IMPORTANT TIPS: A Sunday tour! Journey: Bus 218 (from San Giovanni in Laterano) or Bus 118 (from Metro B: Circo Massimo) to the Catacombs of ❺ San Sebastiano; alternatively: taxi from San Giovanni in Laterano to the church ❷ Quo Vadis (approx. 12 euros) as fewer buses travel at the weekends.

2300 years ago emperors, generals, merchants and columns of legionaries passed along Rome's most important traffic artery which the censor Appicus Claudius Caecus built in 312 BC to the port of Brindisi. Today cars roar along the bumpy road of the ★ Via Appia Antica, which is just 4.30 m/14.1 ft wide. Yet this "Queen of Roads" turns into a virtually traffic-free zone on Sundays and bank holidays (9am–7pm) and becomes the oasis of peace that this archaeological sensation deserves to be – even if not all Romans observe the closure.

10:00am At the ❶ **Information office Via Appia Antica** *(Via Appia Antica 58–60)* you can hire bicycles *(daily 9.30am–4.30pm | tel. 0 65 13 53 16 | www.parcoappiantica.it)* opposite the little church ❷ **Quo Vadis**. According to the legend, St Peter, fleeing from Nero's executioners, encountered Christ here. When he asked "Lord, where are you going?" ("Quo vadis?"), he received the answer "To Rome, to be crucified a second time".

Once you have your bicycle and have adjusted your saddle, **then leave the Via Appia Antica behind you on your left and head straight on along the small private road** over the hill which leads you down to the Catacombs. **A detour onto the Via Ardeatina** takes you first to the ❸ **Calixtus Catacombs** *(Thu–Tue 9am–noon and 2–5pm | admission 8 euros | Via Appia Antica 110–126)* and the ❹ **Domitilla Catacombs** *(Wed–Mon 9am–noon and 2.30–5pm | Via delle Sette Chiese 282 | Via Ardeatina)*. Now ride **along the**

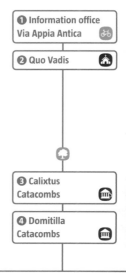

❶ Information office Via Appia Antica

❷ Quo Vadis

❸ Calixtus Catacombs

❹ Domitilla Catacombs

⑤ San Sebastiano fuori le mura 🏠 🏛

⑥ Circo di Massenzio 🏯

⑦ Grave of Romulo 🏯

⑧ Mausoleo di Cecilia Metella 🏯

Via Appia Antica to the Basilica **⑤ San Sebastiano fuori le mura** and to the **Catacombs of San Sebastiano** *(Mon–Sat 9am–noon and 2.30–5pm | admission 8 euros | Via Appia Antica 136).*

12:00pm On your left you can see one of the most splendid archaeological monuments: the **⑥ Circo di Massenzio**, an antique arena, and the **⑦ Grave of Romulo** *(Tue–Sun 10am–4pm)*, not Romulus the founder of the city, but a son of Emperor Maxentius who died young in 309 AD. The most impressive building on the Via Appia is without doubt the battlemented **⑧ Mausoleo di Cecilia Metella**, the grave of a rich Roman wom-

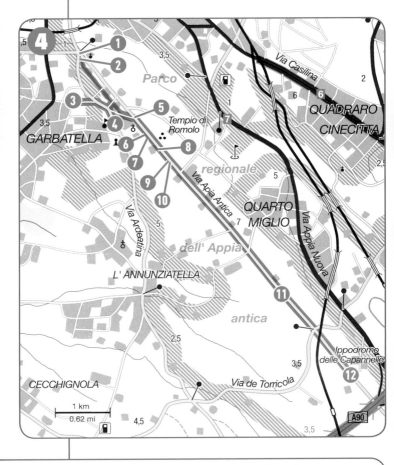

an, daughter of a general. Across from the monument, you'll see a small fountain where you can fill up your water bottles. The first historical section of your tour starts here: Roman cobblestones dating back 2300 years! Tip: Steer your bike wherever possible onto the green verges. And don't forget to note the red stone house on the left in front of the Cecilia Metella monument. If you've not worked up an appetite by now, keep the **⑨ Trattoria "Qui nun se more mai"** *(Tue–Sat noon–11pm, Sun noon–3pm | Via Appia Antica 198 | Budget–Moderate)*, in mind for your return journey. Meaning in English "here you'll never die", you can enjoy authentic Roman cuisine. But maybe a snack is enough to keep you going: at the **⑩ kiosk on the corner of Via C. Metella** you can sit on the wooden benches to eat a panini filled with cheese and ham with a choice of coffee or cold drinks.

`01:00pm` Now comes `INSIDER`**TIP** the most attractive part of the route, beneath pines and cypresses. You pass countless graves – in ancient times burials within the city walls were prohibited – covered with ivy, poppies and daisies. The old Roman paving has also been excavated here. Caesar's carriages had such good suspension – unlike your bicycle's saddle – that the Emperor could travel long distances on the ancient surface in comfort. Another attraction is the nymphaeum of the **⑪ Villa Quintili after approx. km 8**, whose gate is usually locked but is still worth seeing from outside. **After approx. km 10, you'll notice on your left** the arches of the **⑫ Aquedotto Quintili**. Your tour ends here where the old Roman road meets the ring road *Raccordo Anulare* (subway available). On the return stretch, you'll be treated to romantic views of decorated graves, ruins and the Roman *campagna*, which the great German poet Goethe enjoyed so much.

Even Goethe had his picture painted in front of the Mausoleo di Cecilia Metella

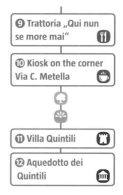

⑨ Trattoria „Qui nun se more mai" 🍴

⑩ Kiosk on the corner Via C. Metella ☕

⑪ Villa Quintili 🏛

⑫ Aquedotto dei Quintili 🏛

5 BY TRAIN TO THE MEDITERRANEAN: OSTIA AND OSTIA ANTICA

START: ❶ Piazzale Ostiense END: ❺ Lido di Castel Fusano	1 day Walking/driving time (without stops) 2 hours
Distance: ➡ 35 km/21.8 mi	

COSTS: Regional train/Metro ticket 1.50 euros a trip, admission ❷ Ostia Antica 8 euros, beach club ❺ **Kursaal** in Ostia with parasol and two loungers 30 euros/2 pers. or free public beach in ❺ **Lido di Castel Fusano**
WHAT TO PACK: water, sun protection, swimwear

IMPORTANT TIPS: During the summer weekends, Ostia is the beach and disco paradise for young Romans. It can get extremely busy!

Take the train back into Ancient Roman times: Ostia Antica, a city of romantic ruins under pine trees less than 30 km/19 mi away from the Eternal City, was once Rome's most important harbour and naval base. Just a few Metro stations further along the train line is Lido di Ostia, Rome's disco and beach paradise.

❶ Piazzale Ostiense

[22 km/13.7 mi]

❷ Ostia Antica

09:00am Take the **regional train to Ostia and Ostia Antica** from ❶ **Piazzale Ostiense** *(Metro B Piramide)*. Get off after approx. 25 minutes at the **Ostia Antica station, cross the Via del Mare over a wooden platform** until you see the entrance of the city of ruins ❷ **Ostia Antica** after approx. 400 m/ 1312 ft. Stroll along the main road **Decumanus Maximus** to **Neptune's thermal baths** (splendid view of the mosaics from the 1st floor), past the **Caserma dei Vigili**, the police and fire station to the **Taverne des Fortunatus** with the 2000-year old saying: "If you're thirsty, drink out of this goblet." Behind the well-preserved **Teatro Romano**, there's the square **INSIDER TIP ▶ Piazzale delle Corporazioni**, where performances are held in summer, you can even see an example of ancient sponsoring: nymphs, sea monsters, dolphins and galleys giving advertising space to the commercial enterprises that financed the theatre

Art in stone: mosaics in Ostia Antica

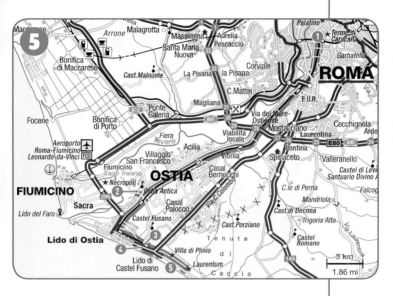

2000 years ago. In contrast to the Forum Romanum or Pompeii, you can almost enjoy Ostia Antica to yourself.

12:00pm Then take the **regional train to the seaside from the Stazione Ostia Antica and get off at the Stazione Castel Fusano in ③ Lido di Ostia**. **④ La Vecchia Pineta** *(daily | Piazzale dell'Aquilone 4 | tel. 06 56 47 02 82 | www. lavecchiapineta.com | Moderate–Expensive)*, is a popular fish restaurant with a terrace overlooking the sea and beach. Now you have to decide how to access the beach: beach access is unfortunately regulated by private 'beach sharks'. The Romans love exclusive beach clubs such as the legendary **Kursaal** *(Lungomare Lutazia Catulo 36 | www.kursaalvillage.com)* and the **Stabilimento Balneare Venezia** *(Lungomare Amerigo Vespucci 8–12 | www.sta bilimentoilvenezia.com)*. A parasol and two loungers will set you back 30 euros for the day but this price includes access to a large swimming pool. Or maybe you prefer to just enjoy refreshment here and **take instead shuttle bus 7 from the train station Cristoforo Colombo heading along the beach promenade to the south** until you spot the dune landscape. Here at the **⑤ Lido di Castel Fusano**, you have free admission to the beaches and the water quality is also better. At km 7.8 there are some small, improvised beach bars.

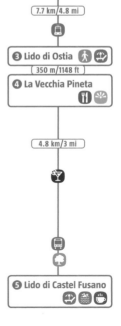

7.7 km / 4.8 mi

③ Lido di Ostia

350 m / 1148 ft

④ La Vecchia Pineta

4.8 km / 3 mi

⑤ Lido di Castel Fusano

TRAVEL WITH KIDS

Is Rome hostile to children? It's like every other big modern city, only a bit more so. The traffic is straight from hell, and there are not many places for running around, as playgrounds are few and far between.

Are the Romans hostile to children? Not in the least. The Italians have so few children themselves that these rarities are cosseted like pandas in the zoo. In a trattoria the kids are stars, and no-one bothers how much mess they make.

Is Rome a good family destination? Yes, if you take a relaxed approach. You don't have to tick the Foro Romano off your list when the temperature is 40 °C/104 °F. And when you go sightseeing, an ice cream or a family photo with the hunky legionaries at the Colosseum (for 5 euros) will put a smile on the face of moaning kids. Show them how to take a drink of water in true Roman style ● INSIDER TIPP from a fontanella, one of the little springs (cover up the jet of water with your hand and position your mouth over the little hole). Even teenagers love Rome if they can go to the flea market at Porta Portese to rummage for cool sunglasses and belts. And how about a bike tour on Via Appia Antica including a visit to the ● catacombs, which also offer shelter from the rain (see page 121)?

BIOPARCO (148 A2) (*M* F4)

The stars in the zoo of Villa Borghese are of course the wolves, Rome's heraldic animals, but there are also 200 other species, from giraffes to lizards. This is a good place for small visitors and big animals. *Daily 9.30am–6pm (summer) 9.30am–5pm (winter), Sat–Sun Apr–Oct until 7pm | admission 16 euros, children above 1m in height 13 euros | Piazzale del Giardino Zoologico 1 | www.bioparco. it | tram 3, 19 | bus 52, 53*

JOIN ASTERIX IN THE FORUM ★

Follow in the footsteps of Asterix on a walk through ancient Rome, taking in the Colosseum and Forum Romanum or the spooky world of the catacombs, or play detective in a historical thriller about Caesar's rise and assassination. The English-language city guides at *Romaculta (mobile tel. 33 87 60 74 70 | www.romaculta.it)* can organise individual tours of Rome for families.

INSIDER TIPP STATUE PARLANTI

Go in search of the odd-looking little figures, eroded by weather and pol-

Lots of ice cream, pizza and fun – Rome has great entertainment for kids, so long as you keep things relaxed

lution, called "talking statues", which performed a democratic function in papal Rome 300 years ago. At night the Pope's subjects could express dissatisfaction with their rulers anonymously through the mouths of the statues. Today still, Romans hang letters and complaints around the neck of *Il Pasquino* (145 C4) *(ꕤ D8)* just beyond Piazza Navona (1164). *Madama Lucrezia* in Palazzetto Venezia (145 E4–5) *(ꕤ E9)* is the only female talking statue. *Abbot Luigi*, on Piazza Vidoni (144 C4) *(ꕤ E9)*, and *Er Facchino*, the porter on Via Lata (145 E4) *(ꕤ E8)*, are quiet figures compared to *Er Babuino*, the baboon. This talkative ape-man squats in the exclusive Via del Babuino, which is named after him, in front of house no. 150 (144 F4) *(ꕤ E6)*.

TEATRO SAN CARLINO (147 F3) *(ꕤ E6)*
On the covered Pincio terrace in the park of Villa Borghese, the San Carlino puppet theatre stages modern puppet musicals and classical Italian puppet theatre with popular characters from Commedia dell'Arte such as Pulcinella and Harlequin. *Ticket reservations: tel. 06 69 92 21 17 or www.sancarlino.it | Viale dei Bambini/corner of Viale Valadier | Metro A Flaminio | bus 117, 119*

VILLA BORGHESE
(148 A–B 2–3) *(ꕤ E–G5)*
Rome's second-biggest park is a wonderful place of recreation for children. You can cycle or take a rickshaw *(hire at Porta Pinciana from 5 euros/hr)*, row a boat on the *laghetto (3 euros/20 min)*, go jogging, have a walk, picnic or use the WiFi to surf on a park bench. For kids from three to ten there is, in addition to the *San Carlino* puppet theatre, the *Casina di Raffaello*, a house for playing in *(Piazza di Siena)*, and a children's cinema. In the *Casina dell'Orologio garden café (Viale dei Bambini 1)* you can enjoy a good buffet. *Via Pinciana | tram 3, 19 | bus 52, 53, 116*

FESTIVALS & EVENTS

Once all the people of Rome went to the seaside in summer. Now the big summer festival *Estate Romana* makes the city attractive too, especially in the evenings.

For the latest programme of events go to the tourist information pavilions, see the daily newspapers (the best source is "Trova Roma" on Thursdays in "La Repubblica", including "The Best in Rome" in English). Information on the internet in English: *www.romaturismo.it, www. abcroma.com, www.romamor.it*

FESTIVALS & EVENTS

JANUARY

On 6 January the white witch *Befana* comes with presents for the children of Rome, and Piazza Navona is turned into a playground.

FEBRUARY

Rome too has its historic *carnevale*, although it's not quite as uninhibited as in Venice.

MARCH/APRIL

Second-but-last Sunday in March: *Rome Marathon (www.maratonadioma.it)* through the Centro Storico.

Urbi et Orbi: on Easter Sunday hundreds of thousands of pilgrims flock to St Peter's Square to receive the Pope's blessing; on Easter Monday *(pasquetta)* they make trips into the countryside.

APRIL

Art fair *Festa d'Arte* in Via Margutta
21 April: *Rome's birthday* with concerts and fireworks

MAY

Festa del Popolo on 1 May, pop concert on Piazza S. Giovanni
Antiques fair in Via dei Coronari (again in September)
Concorso Ippico Internazionale, horse-jumping on Piazza di Siena

JUNE

2 June: *Festa della Repubblica* with a military parade on Via dei Fori Imperiali
13 June: *Feast of St Anthony of Padua* with Mass in Via Merulana
24 June: *S. Giovanni*, fair for St John's day at the Lateran
29 June: *Feast of the city's patrons, St Peter and St Paul*, papal mass in S. Pietro when the faithful kiss the feet of St Peter's statue

Hot Roman nights – concerts in churches, jazz on a piazza and opera in the Baths of Caracalla

JUNE–SEPTEMBER

Estate Romana *(www.estateromana.it)*, Roman summer, with jazz, concerts, open-air cinema and fashion shows

Mondofitness *(www.mondofitness-roma. it)*, big open-air sport and swimming festival in the Tor di Quinto quarter

JULY

INSIDER TIP ***Festa de Noantri***, popular fair in Trastevere with Madonna procession

Tevere Expo, fair of the Italian regions on the bank of the Tiber with music, ballet and folklore, usually until early August

AUGUST

15. Aug: ***Ferragosto***, when you and the stray cats have Rome to yourselves, because many Romans are on holiday

SEPTEMBER

Notte bianca, museum night with concerts, dance, theatre on the 2nd or 3rd Saturday

RomEuropa, festival of music, theatre and dance from states of the EU

NOVEMBER

RomFilmFestival, in the Auditorium Parco della Musica

DECEMBER

8. Dec: ***Feast of the Immaculate Conception*** with prayers by the Pope on Piazza di Spagna

PUBLIC HOLIDAYS

1 Jan	New Year's Day
6 Jan	Epiphany
March/April	Easter Sunday/Monday
25 April	Liberation from Fascism
1 May	Labour Day
2 June	Festival of the Republic
29 June	Peter and Paul
15 Aug	Assumption of the Virgin
1 Nov	All Saints' Day
8 Dec	Immaculate Conception
25/26 Dec	Christmas

LINKS, BLOGS, APPS & MORE

LINKS & BLOGS

www.viator.com Promises classic tours through Rome without having to queue, for example at the Vatican museums and St. Peter's Basilica from 35 euros

www.discotechearoma.it Geared towards young Romans: up-to-the-minute tips on Rome's clubbing scene as well as jazz and concerts

www.listicket.it Are you looking for a ticket for a concert, a football match or the JazzTram, a high-class evening meal in a restored historic tram? Book here online (English version available).

www.ticketone.it Tickets for concerts, sporting activities, events, English version available

www.spottedbylocals.com/rome Five young Roman media professionals have put their recommendations for restaurants, nightlife and events online, paying attention to the less-known quarters of the city. Here are some addresses that don't feature elsewhere, including some places that are hard to find

www.facebook.com/pages/Rome/27359671110 Link to the Facebook group "Rome". Lots of tips, details of events, news and much more about Rome.

katieparla.com/blog The best and funniest US-American food blogger Katie Parla from New Jersey has been living in Rome for 13 years. By now, she offers also tours and has published her own food app

www.timeout.com/rome Plenty of tips and advice, event information, what's on at the cinemas and theatres in English

Regardless of whether you are still preparing your trip or already in Rome: these addresses will provide you with more information, videos and networks to make your holiday even more enjoyable

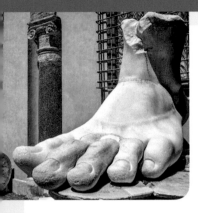

short.travel/rom1 3D reconstruction of Rome in the late Antiquity (320 AD). The camera drone lets you fly over the Forum Romanum, Colosseum, Circus Maximus and other classical buildings and monuments

short.travel/rom2 Omaggio a Roma – director Franco Zeffirelli's ravishing short video about Rome with arias by Andrea Bocelli and appearances by Monica Bellucci.

short.travel/rom3 Get a insider's view of Zaha Hadid's ultra-modern MAXXI museum. This five-minute video introduces the bold architecture of the new museum of contemporary art.

Learn Italian Words Free Flashcard dictionary with 10,000 words and phrases at different levels of difficulty. With audio pronunciation

Roma Capitale Information about the city of Rome: street maps, bus routes, hotels, restaurants, attractions and even the weather. Suitable for iPhone and Android, in Italian only

TRAVEL TIPS

ARRIVAL

✈ Rome has two airports. Scheduled flights, e.g. Alitalia from London and New York, British Airways from London, go to Leonardo da Vinci airport in Fiumicino, which lies 32 km/20 mi outside Rome. Charter and budget airlines such as Ryanair and Easyjet land at Ciampino, about 18 km/11 mi southeast of Rome.

Leonardo da Vinci: a taxi into the city centre costs about 50 euros, there is a surcharge for the suburbs. It is faster and cheaper to take the *Leonardo-Express (14 euros, tickets from the ticket machines in front of the platform in the airport train station | from the airport 6.23am–11.23pm every 30 min., from Stazione Termini (platform 25) 5.35am–10.35pm every 30 min.).*

Ciampino: a taxi to the city centre costs approx. 35 euros. Some airlines provide a bus service to Stazione Termini for 8 euros. The city buses of Atral will even take you there for 4 euros every hour from 7.25am. Every 20 minutes, Terravision buses go from Fiumicino (stop in front of terminal 3) as well as from Ciampino to Stazione Termini, Via Marsala 29 (in front of platform 1).

🚗 Autostrada del Sole leads to the Grande Raccordo Anulare (G.R.A.), Rome's orbital motorway. Follow the signs for Roma centro; otherwise you end up in the suburbs!

🚆 Most trains arrive at Stazione Termini. The trains that carry holidaymakers' cars stop at Stazione Tiburtina.

BANKS

All banks (banca) and savings banks (cassa di risparmio) have cashpoints (ATMs) and usually open Mon–Fri 8.30am–3 or 4pm.

BIKES & MOPEDS

Cycle and moped hire is becoming increasingly popular e.g.: Roma rent a bike (144 C5) (*DD D9*) *(Via di San Paolo alla Regola 33/at Campo de' Fiori | tel. 06 88 92 23 65 | www.romarentbike.com), Roma rent a Scooter (144 C4) (DD D9) (Via del Paradiso 42/near Corso Vittorio Emanuele II | tel. 0 66 83 22 22 | www.romarentscooter.com) or Bici e baci (148 B–C5) (DD G–H7) (Via del Viminale 5 | www.bicibaci.com) or Via Cavour 302 (152 A2) (DD F–G9).* Bici e Baci also hire vespas or organizes cycle tours, e.g. along the Via Appia Antica.

RESPONSIBLE TRAVEL

It doesn't take a lot to be environmentally friendly whilst travelling. Don't just think about your carbon footprint whilst flying to and from your holiday destination but also about how you can protect nature and culture abroad. As a tourist it is especially important to respect nature, look out for local products, cycle instead of driving, save water and much more. If you would like to find out more about ecotourism please visit: *www.ecotourism.org*

From arrival to weather

Holiday from start to finish: the most important addresses and information for your trip to Rome

If you would like to hire an electric bike, then head for *Ecovia Bici eletriche* (152 A1) *(ﬃ G9) (Via Cardello 32 | tel. 06 45 50 89 23 | www.ecovia.it)*.

Segways can now be hired at various stations around Rome for approx. 15 euros an hour, for example at the entrance to the large Villa Borghese park (148 A3–4) *(ﬃ F6)*. A three-hour classic tour of Rome costs approx. 80 euros *(www.romebysegway.com)*.

CONSULATES & EMBASSIES

BRITISH EMBASSY
Via XX Settembre 80a / 00187 Roma RM / tel. 06 4220 0001 / http://ukinitaly.fco.gov.uk/en/

U.S. EMBASSY ROME
Via Vittorio Veneto 121 / 00187 Rome, Italy / tel. 06 46741 / https://it.usembassy.gov/embassy-consulates/embassy/

CUSTOMS

Unlimited goods for personal use can be imported and exported without paying duties within states of the European Union. If you come from outside the EU, the duty-free allowances are: 1 litre of spirits or 2 litres of sparkling wine or 2 litres of fortified wine, and 4 litres of non-sparkling wine; 200 cigarettes or 250 grams of smoking tobacco or 100 cigarillos or 50 cigars, plus other goods with a maximum total value of 430 euros.

DRIVING

Italy's traffic regulations have become stricter, and fines are steep. The maximum blood alcohol level is 0.5%. Seat belts must be worn, and moped riders must have a helmet. The speed limit on three-lane motorways is 130 km/h/80 mph (110 km/h/68 mph if it rains). Outside built-up areas cars must drive with their lights on. Remember to have a fluorescent jacket, in case of a breakdown when leaving the car outside built-up areas – the fine for not having one is 137 euros.

EMERGENCY

Police (Carabinieri): tel. 112, 113
Fire brigade: tel. 115
ACI breakdown service: tel. 116
Stolen cars: *Questura* (148 B6) *(ﬃ G8) (Via Genova 2 | tel. 0 64 68 61)*, where interpreters are available, or the nearest police or Carabinieri station.

GUIDED TOURS

Personal guided tours or double-decker bus tours are a great way to see Rome's attractions.

BUS TO VIA APPIA
The best route is to take bus 218 from Piazza di Porta San Giovanni in Laterano (152 C3) *(ﬃJ10) (Metro A San Giovanni)* to Via Appia Antica. Bus 118 also travels from Piazzale Ostiense (143 E–F5) *(ﬃ F13) (Metro B Piramide)* As only a handful of buses travel on Sundays, it is advisable to take a taxi.

ROME OPEN TOUR – PINK DOUBLE-DECKER
You're probably familiar with the "hop-on, hop-off" principle from other city

breaks: you pay once and you can hop on and off anytime. *Daily departures 9am–7pm every 20 min, Nov–mid-March 9am–5pm | Piazza Cinquecento (Stazione Termini)* (148 C5) *(⫘ H8) | 20 euros/24 hrs or 24 euros/48 hrs. | www.romeopentour.it*

ROMA CRISTIANA – PILGRIM LINES

The double-decker buses run by the Roman pilgrim organisation take you to the seven pilgrimage churches and other Roman Catholic sights. *Daily 9.30am–6pm | Via della Conciliazione (St Peter's Square)* (146 B5) *(⫘ B7) | ticket to hop on and off 20 euros/24 hrs or 23 euros/48 hrs. | www.operaroman apellegrinaggi.org*

THROUGH ETERNITY TOURS

Sophisticated personal city tours by art-historians and archaeologists – to Rome's underworld and on the trail of Caravaggio. *Tel. 06 700 93 39 | www.througheternity.com*

ROMACULTA

Art-historians and archaeologists show you the city on wonderful individual guided walks, e. g. Roman Landmarks, Baroque Walks and Art in the Vatican. *Tel. 33 73 71 15 46 | www.romaculta.it*

ROMAMIRABILIA

City tours with German art-historians, as well as cookery classes, gourmet or vespa tours and incentive-building workshops for corporate groups. *Tel. 06 45 49 73 72 | www.romamirabilia.com*

HEALTH

Emergencies and ambulance: *tel. 118* 24-hour pharmacy:
Farmacia Internazionale (140 C5) *(⫘ H8) (Piazza dei Cinquecento 51 | Stazi-*

one Termini and Via Cola di Rienzo 213 (146 B4) *(⫘ C6)*
First aid *(pronto soccorso)* is free of charge in all hospitals. For citizens of the EU, the European insurance card EHIC entitles you to treatment (sometimes with additional fees). Visitors from North America and other non-EU countries should take out private insurance. Children's hospital: *Ospedale dei Bambini* (150 B1) *(⫘ B8) (Piazza S. Onofrio | tel. 0 66 85 91).*

HOLIDAY TIMES

Many hotels, restaurants and shops are closed in early January and in the Italian holiday season, i.e. in August (Ferragosto).

INFORMATION BEFORE YOU GO

ITALIAN STATE TOURIST BOARD
– 1, Princes Street | London W1B 2AY | tel. 020 74 08 12 54 | www.enit.it
– 630 Fifth Avenue – Suite 1965 / New York, New York 10111 / tel. 212 245-5618 / www.enit.it
– Ground Floor, 140 William Street | East Sydney NSW 2011 | Australia | tel. 02 9357 2561 | www.enit.it

INFORMATION IN ROME

INFO LINE & INFO PAVILIONS
The tourist authorities run an information service: tel. 06 06 08 for information in English about public transport, events and opening hours *(see also www.rome.info).*
There are also tourist information pavilions *(9.30am–7pm)*: Castel Sant'Angelo *(Piazza Pia)* (146 C5) *(⫘ C7)*; Corso *(Via Minghetti)* (145 E3) *(⫘ E8)*; Via dei Fori Imperiali *(opposite Forum Romanum)* (152 A2) *(⫘ F9)*; Stazione

Termini *(by platform 24, entrance also from Via Giolitti 34)* (148 C6) *(ﬗ J8)*; Piazza Cinque Lune *(near Piazza Navona)* (144 C3)*(ﬗ D8)*; Via Nazionale *(Palazzo Esposizioni)* (148 B6) *(ﬗ G8)*

TOURING CLUB ITALIANO

(147 F6) *(ﬗ F8)* Advice for drivers, including traffic updates. *Mon–Sat 10am–7pm | Piazza Santi Apostoli 22 | tel. 06 36 00 52 81 | www.touringclub.it | bus 280*

RAILWAYS (FS)

(148 C5)*(ﬗ H8)* Timetable information tel. 89 20 21 | www.ferroviedellostato. it, reservations via travel agents in Rome and in Stazione Termini.

INTERNET & WIFI

The large hotels have WiFi – *rete senza fili* in Italian – but normally charge for it. Thanks to **INSIDER TIP** *www.digitroma. com* (online registration necessary) you can surf free of charge for up to four hours a day at many of the nicest city squares and in many parks. Additionally they provide a lot of up to date tips on Rome.Favoured cafés with a WiFi service: *The Library (Vicolo della Cancelleria 7 | www. thelibrary.it), Café Friends (Piazza Trilussa 34) or Good Bar (Via di San Dorotea 8–9)*.

LOST & FOUND

The city's lost property office *(Ufficio degli Oggetti Rinvenuti)* is in the *Circonvallazione Ostiense* 191 (154 C5) *(ﬗ F14)* (Mon–Fri 8.30am–1pm, Thu until 5pm | tel. 06 67 69 32 14 | www.oggettismarriti@ comune.roma.it | Metro B Garbatella)*.

PAPAL AUDIENCES

When the Pope is in Rome, he holds a general audience on St Peter's Square

BUDGETING

Espresso	0.80 £/1 $
	standing at the counter
Ice cream	2.65 £/3.35 $
	for a large portion
Panino	3.50–5.30 £/4.50–6.70 $
	for a large filled panino
T-Shirt	9 £/11 $
	for a souvenir T-shirt
Bus	1.30 £/1.70 $
	for a single journey
Disco	from 17.50 £/22.50 $
	admission per person

on Wednesdays at 10.30am and says the Angelus prayer from the window of the Vatican Palace on Sundays at 12 noon *(www.vatican.va)*. Tickets for papal audiences are free. You can pick them up the previous day (not sooner) directly from the Swiss Guards at the "Bronze Door" *(3pm–7pm in summer, 3pm–6pm in winter)*. Pre-booking or reservation, which is obligatory if you need more than 10 tickets, is possible via fax. For detailed information and the ticket request form have a look at: *www.papalaudience.org/ tickets*

PHONE & MOBILE PHONE

To phone home, the code is 0044 for UK, 00353 for Ireland, then the local code without the first 0. The country code for the USA and Canada is 001. When phoning Italy from abroad, the code is 0039 – followed by the local code including the 0. The Italian word for mobile phone is cellulare or telefonino. You'll get a signal everywhere in Rome, usually from the TIM *(Telecom Italiana Mobile)* network. If you want to use a landline, it's best to buy a phone card *(carta telecom no* distance) for 5, 10 or 20 euros at a tobacconist's *(tabacchi)* and make the call from a public phone.

All phone numbers in Rome start with 06 – whether you make a call from within the city, from somewhere else in Italy or from abroad. Only Italian mobile phones don't have a 0 first. But in Rome – the same as in other locations – you now have to look a little longer to find a public telephone.

PUBLIC TRANSPORT

Many bus routes are literally cancelled or restarted overnight due to the crisis. Especially at the weekends there are fewer trams, buses and Metro trains travelling. Up-to-date information available at www.atac.roma.it. A BIT ticket for bus or Metro costs 1.50 euros *(single trip, valid for 100 min)*, a day ticket 6 euros (3 days 16.50 euros, 7 days 24 euros). Buy them from an office of ATAC (the transport authority), e.g. in front of Stazione Termini (148 C5) *(Ⓜ H8)*, Piazza San Silvestro (145 E2) *(Ⓜ E7)* or at one of the many tobacconists and kiosks with the black, red and yellow *ATAC* sign. The tickets have to be stamped in the bus, Metro or tram!

Rome has only two Metro lines. *Linea A:* Battistini to Anagnina (south-eastern suburb, towards Castelli Romani) and Linea B: Rebibbia to EUR-Laurentina and Linea B1: Piazza Bologna to Conca d'Oro. They run *Sun–Thu 5.30am–11.30pm, Fri/Sat 5.30–1.30am.* There are ticket machines at station entrances.

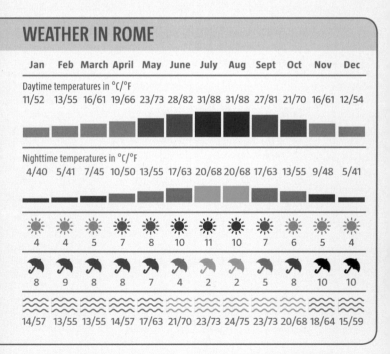

WEATHER IN ROME

	Jan	Feb	March	April	May	June	July	Aug	Sept	Oct	Nov	Dec
Daytime temperatures in °C/°F	11/52	13/55	16/61	19/66	23/73	28/82	31/88	31/88	27/81	21/70	16/61	12/54
Nighttime temperatures in °C/°F	4/40	5/41	7/45	10/50	13/55	17/63	20/68	20/68	17/63	13/55	9/48	5/41
Sunshine hours/day	4	4	5	7	8	10	11	10	7	6	5	4
Precipitation days/month	8	9	8	8	7	4	2	2	5	8	10	10
Water temperature in °C/°F	14/57	13/55	13/55	14/57	17/63	21/70	23/73	24/75	23/73	20/68	18/64	15/59

ROMA PASS

For 38.50 euros the *Roma Pass (www. romapass.it)* gives you use of the Metro lines and all buses for three days (Roma Pass for two days: 28 euros), free admission to two museums of your choice without queuing (not valid for the Vatican Museums) and discounts for other museums and exhibitions. The pass is on sale at all tourist information kiosks, ATAC offices, in Stazione Termini and at Fiumicino airport. The *Archeologia Card* (23 euros) allows you to enter the Colosseum, the Palatin, the Museo Nazionale Romano, the Terme di Caracalla and two museums along the Via Appia Antica. It is valid for seven days and can be purchased in the museums.

TABACCHI-SHOPS

The Romans love their *tabacchi* as they not only sell cigarettes, but also bus tickets, stamps, telephone cards and many more things. Look out for the black sign, attached mostly to housewalls, depicting a white "T".

TAXI

Taxi trips are not cheap, but the taximeters are calibrated properly and checked. The basic price is 3 euros. Supplements: night rate from 10pm 6.50 euros, Sundays and holidays 4.50 euros. The first 10 km/6.2 mi cost 1.10 euros, from then on 1.30–1.60 euros. The first piece of luggage is free, 1 euro for every further piece. From Fiumicino Airport expect to pay approx. 50 euros to the city centre, from Ciampino 35 euros. *Tel. 06 49 94, 06 66 45, 06 35 70.*

THEFT

If you are a victim of theft, notify the nearest police or Carabinieri station or the *Questura* (police administration). Interpreters are available to record the details. *Via San Vitale 1* (148 B6) *(𝄢 G8)* | *tel. 0 64 68 61 | Metro A Repubblica | bus 60, 64, 70, 7*

TIPPING

Here are some suggestions for the right amount: porters get 1 euro per bag, chambermaids 1 euro per night or 3 euros per week, a hotel porter 1 euro. Give waiters 5–10 per cent depending on how satisfied you were. Taxi drivers expect nothing, but you can round up the amount if you're happy with the service.

CURRENCY CONVERTER

£	€	€	£
1	1.15	1	0.88
3	3.45	3	2.64
5	5.75	5	4.40
13	14.95	13	11.44
40	46	40	35.20
75	86.25	75	66
120	138	120	105.60
250	287.50	250	220
500	575	500	440

$	€	€	$
1	0.90	1	1.10
3	2.70	3	3.30
5	4.50	5	5.50
13	11.70	13	14.30
40	36	40	44
75	67.50	75	82.50
120	108	120	132
250	225	250	275
500	450	500	550

For current exchange rates see www.xe.com

USEFUL PHRASES ITALIAN

PRONUNCIATION

c, cc	before e or i like ch in "church", e.g. ciabatta, otherwise like k
ch, cch	like k, e.g. pacchi, che
g, gg	before e or i like j in "just", e.g. gente, otherwise like g in "get"
gl	like "lli" in "million", e.g. figlio
gn	as in "cognac", e.g. bagno
sc	before e or i like sh, e.g. uscita
sch	like sk in "skill", e.g. Ischia
z	at the beginning of a word like dz in "adze", otherwise like ts

An accent on an Italian word shows that the stress is on the last syllable.
In other cases we have shown which syllable is stressed by placing a dot below the relevant vowel.

IN BRIEF

Yes/No/Maybe	Sì/No/Forse
Please/Thank you	Per favore/Grazie
Excuse me, please!	Scusa!/Mi scusi
May I ...?/Pardon?	Posso ...? / Come dice?/Prego?
Good morning!/Good afternoon!/	Buon giorno!/Buon giorno!/
Good evening!/Good night!	Buona sera!/Buona notte!
Hello! / Goodbye!/See you	Ciao!/Salve! / Arrivederci!/Ciao!
My name is ...	Mi chiamo ...
What's your name?	Come si chiama?/Come ti chiami
I would like to .../Have you got ...?	Vorrei .../Avete ...?
How much is ...?	Quanto costa ...?
I (don't) like that	(Non) mi piace
good/bad	buono/cattivo
broken/doesn't work	guasto/non funziona
too much/much/little/all/nothing	troppo/molto/poco/tutto/niente
Help!/Attention!/Caution!	aiuto!/attenzione!/prudenza!
ambulance/police/fire brigade	ambulanza/polizia/vigili del fuoco
Prohibition/forbidden	divieto/vietato
danger/dangerous	pericolo/pericoloso

DATE & TIME

Monday/Tuesday/Wednesday	lunedì/martedì/mercoledì
Thursday/Friday/Saturday	giovedì/venerdì/sabato

Parli italiano?

'Do you speak Italian?' This guide will help you to
say the basic words and phrases in Italian.

Sunday/holiday/	domenica/(giorno) festivo
working day	(giorno) feriale
today/tomorrow/yesterday	oggi/domani/ieri
hour/minute	ora/minuto
week/month/year	settimana/mese/anno
What time is it?	Che ora è? Che ore sono?
It's three o'clock/It's half past three	Sono le tre/Sono le tre e mezza
a quarter to four/	le quattro meno un quarto/
a quarter past four	un quarto alle quattro

TRAVEL

open/closed	aperto/chiuso
entrance/exit	entrata/uscita
departure/arrival	partenza/arrivo
toilets/ladies/gentlemen	bagno/signore/signori
(no) drinking water	acqua (non) potabile
Where is ...?/Where are ...?	Dov'è ...?/Dove sono ...?
left/right/straight ahead/back	sinistra/destra/dritto/indietro
close/far	vicino/lontano
bus/tram	bus/tram
taxi	taxi/tassì
bus stop/taxi stand	fermata/posteggio taxi
parking lot/parking garage	parcheggio/parcheggio coperto
street map/map	pianta/mappa
train station/harbour/airport	stazione/porto/aeroporto
schedule/ticket/supplement	orario/biglietto/supplemento
single/return	solo andata/andata e ritorno
train/track/platform	treno/binario/banchina
I would like to rent ...	Vorrei noleggiare ...
a car/a bicycle/boat	una macchina/una bicicletta/una barca
petrol/gas station	distributore/stazione di servizio
petrol/gas / diesel	benzina/diesel/gasolio
breakdown/repair shop	guasto/officina

FOOD & DRINK

Could you please book a table for tonight for four?	Vorrei prenotare per stasera un tavolo per quattro?
on the terrace/by the window	sulla terrazza/ vicino alla finestra
The menu, please	Il menù, per favore
bottle/carafe/glass	bottiglia/caraffa/bicchiere

knife/fork/spoon	coltello/forchetta/cucchiaio
salt/pepper/sugar	sale/pepe/ zucchero
vinegar/oil/milk/cream/lemon	aceto/olio/latte/panna/limone
cold/too salty/not cooked	freddo/troppo salato/non cotto
with/without ice/sparkling	con/senza ghiaccio/gas
vegetarian/allergy	vegetariano/vegetariana/allergia
May I have the bill, please?	Vorrei pagare/Il conto, per favore
bill/tip	conto/mancia

SHOPPING

Where can I find...?	Dove posso trovare ...?
I'd like .../I'm looking for ...	Vorrei .../Cerco ...
Do you put photos onto CD?	Vorrei masterizzare delle foto su CD?
pharmacy	farmacia
baker/market	forno/ mercato
shopping centre/department store	centro commerciale/grandemagazzino
grocery	negozio alimentare
supermarket	supermercato
photographic items/newspaper shop	articoli per foto/giornalaio
100 grammes/1 kilo	un etto/un chilo
expensive/cheap/price	caro/economico/prezzo
organically grown	di agricoltura biologica

ACCOMMODATION

Do you have any ... left?	Avete ancora ...
single room/double room	una (camera) singola/doppia
breakfast/half board/ full board	prima colazione/mezza pensione/
(American plan)	pensione completa
at the front/seafront/lakefront	con vista/con vista sul mare/lago
shower/sit-down bath/balcony/terrace	doccia/bagno/balcone/terrazza
key/room card	chiave/scheda magnetica
luggage/suitcase/bag	bagaglio/valigia/borsa

BANKS, MONEY & CREDIT CARDS

bank/ATM/pin code	banca/bancomat/ codice segreto
cash/credit card	in contanti/carta di credito
bill/coin/change	banconota/moneta/il resto

HEALTH

doctor/dentist/paediatrician	medico/dentista/pediatra
hospital/emergency clinic	ospedale/pronto soccorso
fever/pain	febbre/dolori

diarrhoea/nausea/sunburn	diarrea/nausea/scottatura solare
inflamed/injured	infiammato/ferito
plaster/bandage/ointment/cream	cerotto/fasciatura/pomata/crema
pain reliever/tablet/suppository	antidolorifico/compressa/supposta

TELECOMMUNICATIONS & MEDIA

stamp/letter/postcard	francobollo/lettera/cartolina
I need a landline phone card	Mi serve una scheda telefonica per la rete fissa
I'm looking for a prepaid card for my mobile	Cerco una scheda prepagata per il mio cellulare
Where can I find internet access?	Dove trovo un accesso internet?
dial/connection/engaged	comporre/linea/occupato
socket/adapter/charger	presa/riduttore/caricabatterie
computer/battery/rechargeable battery	computer/batteria/accumulatore
"at" (@) sign	chiocciola
internet address (URL)/e-mail address	indirizzo internet/indirizzo email
internet connection/wifi	collegamento internet/wi-fi
e-mail/file/print	email/file/stampare

LEISURE, SPORTS & BEACH

beach/bathing beach	spiaggia/bagno/stabilimento balneare
sunshade/lounger/cable car/chair lift	ombrellone/sdraio/funivia/seggiovia
(rescue) hut/avalanche	rifugio/valanga

NUMBERS

0	zero	17	diciassette
1	uno	18	diciotto
2	due	19	diciannove
3	tre	20	venti
4	quattro	21	ventuno
5	cinque	30	trenta
6	sei	40	quaranta
7	sette	50	cinquanta
8	otto	60	sessanta
9	nove	70	settanta
10	dieci	80	ottanta
11	undici	90	novanta
12	dodici	100	cento
13	tredici	1000	mille
14	quattordici	2000	duemila
15	quindici	½	un mezzo
16	sedici	¼	un quarto

STREET ATLAS

The green line indicates the Discovery Tour "Rome at a glance"
The blue line indicates the other Discovery Tours
All tours are also marked on the pull-out map

Exploring Rome

The map on the back cover shows how
the area has been sub-divided

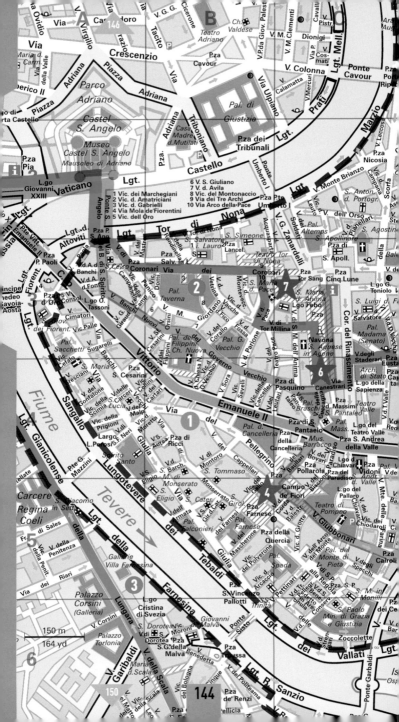

Via Ovidio V. G.G. Cicerone Via V. Cavalli V. Pistr.

A V. Cadoro 146 B Ch. Valdese V. Giov. Palest.

Via Tacito V. M. Clementi V. M. Dionigi

Via Virgilio Orazio Teatro Adriano V. P. da Giov. Palest. V. Cosmati V. P. Pza Cavour V. Colonna Ponte Cavour Pza. V. R.

Crescenzio Piazza Adriana Prati Lgt. Mell.

Maria d. Cam. Valle Parco Adriano Piazza Adriana Pal. di Giustizia V. Calamatta V.Mercuri Ponte Cavour Pza. V. R.

erico II Piazza Castello S. Angelo Casa Madre d.Mutilati Pza dei Tribunali Marzio V. Lecosti

go di ta Castello Museo Castel S. Angelo Mausoleo di Adriano Ponte Umberto I Lgt. Pza Nicosia Scorfa

Pza Pia L.go Giovanni XXIII Vaticano Lgt. Castello 6 V. S. Giuliano 7 V. d. Avila 8 Vic. del Montonaccio 9 Via dei Tre Archi 10 Via Arco della Pace

1 Vic. dei Marchegiani 2 Vic. d. Amatriciani 3 Vic. d. Gabrielli 4 Via Mola de'Fiorentini 5 Vic. dell'Oro

Lgt. Altoviti Lgt. Tor di Nona S. Salvatore S. Simeone Acquasparta S. Anton. d. Portogh. S. Agostino

Lgt. Vaticano Ponte S. Angelo Tor di Nona S. Salvatore S. Apollinare Pza di S. Agostino

P.za Paoli Banchi Coronari Via dei Coronari 10 S. Maria d. Pace 7 Lgo Febo S. Luigi d. Franc.

incipe savoia-Aosta Pza S. d'Oro Consol. L.go Tassoni 2 Pal. Taverna Pza Navona in Agone 6 Cor. del Rinascimento Pal. Madama (Senato)

Fiume Tevere Lungotevere Sangallo Vittorio Emanuele II Pza del Pasquino Pza Navona 4 Campo de' Fiori Teatro di Pompeo

150 m 164 yd Palazzo Corsini (Galleria) Farnesina Lungara Palazzo Torlonia S. Dorotea Pza Trilussa Ponte Sisto Lgt. dei Vallati

6 150 Garibaldi V. della Scala 144 de' Renzi Pza V.R. Sanzio Ponte R. Sanzio

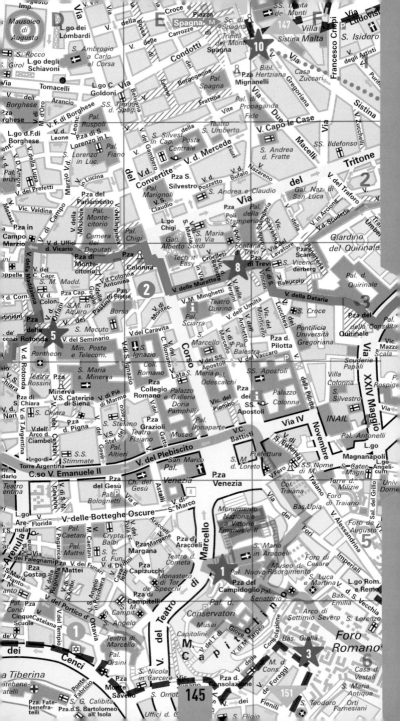

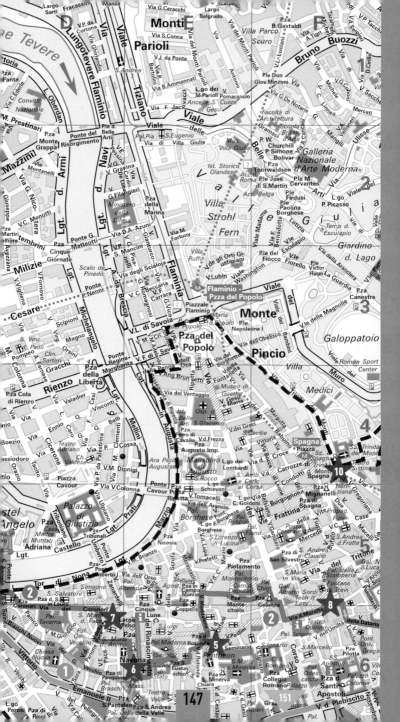

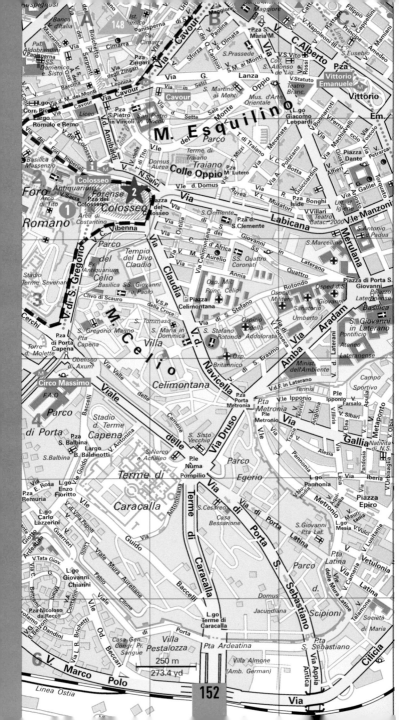

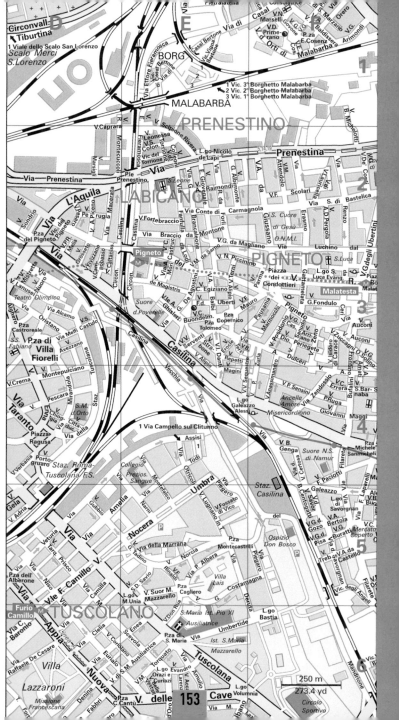

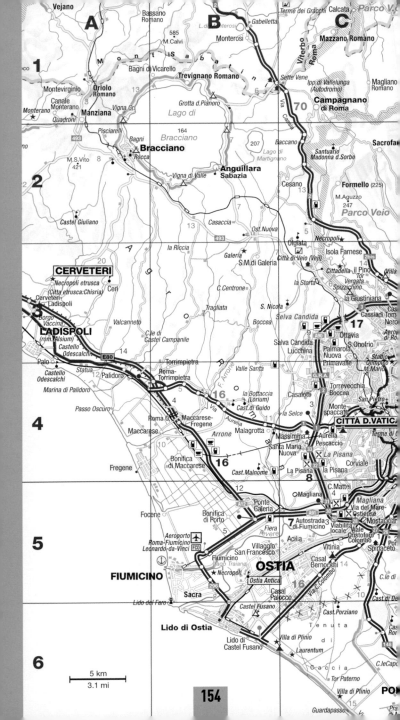

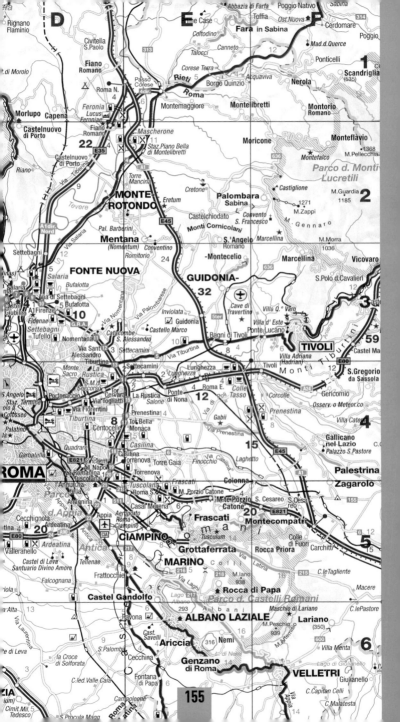

155

The index includes a selection of the streets and squares shown in the street atlas

KEY TO STREET ATLAS

Autostrada / Autobahn		Motorway / Autoroute
Strada a quattro corsie / Vierspurige Straße		Road with four lanes / Route à quatre voies
Strada di attraversamento / Durchgangsstraße		Thoroughfare / Route de transit
Strada principale / Hauptstraße		Main road / Route principale
Altre strade / Sonstige Straßen		Other roads / Autres routes
Informazioni / Information	**i**	Information / Information
Parcheggio / Parkplatz	**P**	Parking place / Parking
Ostello della gioventù / Jugendherberge	▲	Youth hostel / Auberge de jeunesse
Via a senso unico / Einbahnstraße		One-way street / Rue à sens unique
Zona pedonale / Fußgängerzone		Pedestrian zone / Zone piétonne
Ferrovia principale con stazione / Hauptbahn mit Bahnhof		Main railway with station / Chemin de fer principal avec gare
Altra ferrovia / Sonstige Bahn		Other railway / Autre ligne
Metropolitana / U-Bahn	Ⓜ·····	Underground / Métro
Tram / Straßenbahn		Tramway / Tramway
Chiesa - Chiesa interessante / Kirche - Sehenswerte Kirche		Church - Church of interest / Église - Église remarquable
Sinagoga / Synagoge		Synagogue / Synagogue
Ufficio postale - Posto di polizia / Postamt - Polizeistation		Post office - Police station / Bureau de poste - Poste de police
Monumento - Torre / Denkmal - Turm		Monument - Tower / Monument - Tour
Ospedale - Autobus per l'aeroporto / Krankenhaus - Flughafenbus	⊕ **B**	Hospital - Airport bus / Hôpital - Bus d'aéroport
Caseggiato, edificio pubblico / Bebaute Fläche, öffentliches Gebäude		Built-up area, public building / Zone bâtie, bâtiment public
Zona industriale - Parco, bosco / Industriegelände - Park, Wald		Industrial area - Park, forest / Zone industrielle - Parc, bois
Cimitero - Cimitero ebraico / Friedhof - Jüdischer Friedhof		Cemetery - Jewish cemetery / Cimetière - Cimetière juif
Confine della città / Stadtgrenze		Municipal boundary / Limite municipale
Zona con limitazioni di traffico / Zone mit Verkehrsbeschränkungen	⊏ ⊐ ⊏	Restricted traffic zone / Circulation réglementée par des péages
Giro avventura 1 / MARCO POLO Erlebnistour 1		MARCO POLO Discovery Tour 1 / MARCO POLO Tour d'aventure 1
Giri avventurosi / MARCO POLO Erlebnistouren		MARCO POLO Discovery Tours / MARCO POLO Tours d'aventure
MARCO POLO Highlight	★	MARCO POLO Highlight

MARCO POLO TRAVEL GUIDES

INDEX

All sights and destinations mentioned in this guide as well as some important streets and squares are listed in this index. Page numbers in bold refer to the main entry.

CREDITS

WRITE TO US

e-mail: info@marcopologuides.co.uk
Did you have a great holiday?
Is there something on your mind?
Whatever it is, let us know!
Whether you want to praise, alert us to errors or give us a personal tip – MARCO POLO would be pleased to hear from you.
We do everything we can to provide the very latest information for your trip.

Nevertheless, despite all of our authors' thorough research, errors can creep in. MARCO POLO does not accept any liability for this. Please contact us by e-mail or post.
MARCO POLO Travel Publishing Ltd
Pinewood, Chineham Business Park
Crockford Lane, Chineham
Basingstoke, Hampshire RG24 8AL
United Kingdom

PICTURE CREDITS
Cover photograph: Piazza Navona (Schapowalow: R. Spila)
Photos: CampoMarzio70/Design for Architecture (19 below); DuMont Bildarchiv: Zoltan Nagy (17, 57, 69, 120, 126/127, 130 below); R. Freyer (flap right, 5, 20/21, 79, 107, 126, 127); Getty Images/Archivio J. Lange/Kontributor: Dea (38); huber-images: Albanese (48), Bernhart (23), U. Bernhart (19 top), M. Carassale (66), C. Cassaro (110/111), G. Croppi (72), Gräfenhain (flap left, 11), Hallberg (62), S. Kremer (2, 12/13, 26/27, 44/45, 47, 61, 130 top, 131), J. Lawrence (14/15), M. Mastorillo (70/71, 84), Zoltan Nagy (65, 96), A. Piai (31), B. Pipe (3), Rellini (52/53), M. Rellini (4 below), J. Ritterbach (39), N. Russo (32), A. Saffo (142/143), S. Scatà (75), Serrano (6, 128), A. Serrano (10, 37, 42), Spila (98/99); Laif: A. Faccilongo (94), Heuer (100/101), G. Kloetzer (117), E. Paoni (92/93); Laif/contrasto: M. Siragusa (102); Laif/A3: A. Casasoli (129); Laif/A3/contrasto: A. Cristofari (50/51); Laif/Hemis.fr: R. Mattes (89); Laif/Polaris: I. Benotto (128/129); Look: Pompe (7, 40); Look/age fotostock (108); Lookphotos: M. Hoffmann (105), I. Pompe (58); mauritius images: Mattes (9), J. Warburton-Lee (124); mauritius images/Alamy (18 top, 22, 76, 78 right, 81, 87, 90, 123); mauritius images/CuboImages (82/83); mauritius images/Image Source (18 below); mauritius images/imagebroker: Handl (8), M. Jung (35); mauritius images/PACIFIC PRESS/Alamy: M. Nardone (18 centre); mauritius images/United Archives (25); H. Pabel (1 below); Schapowalow: R. Spila (1 top); T. Stankiewicz (4 top, 55, 78 left)

4th edition – fully revised and updated 2018
Worldwide Distribution: Marco Polo Travel Publishing Ltd., Pinewood; Chineham Business Park, Crockford Lane, Basingstoke, Hampshire RG24 8AL, UK. Email: sales@marcopolouk.com
© MAIRDUMONT GmbH & Co.KG, Ostfildern
Chief editor: Marion Zorn
Author: Swantje Strieder; editor: Marlis v. Hessert-Fraatz; programme supervision: Lucas Forst-Gill, Susanne Heimburger, Nikolai Michaelis, Martin Silbermann, Kristin Wittemann
Picture editor: Stefanie Wiese, Gabriele Forst; cartography street atlas: © MAIRDUMONT, Ostfildern; cartography pull-out map: © MAIRDUMONT, Ostfildern
Cover design, p. 1, pull-out map cover: Karl Anders – Büro für Visual Stories, Hamburg; design inside: milchhof:atelier, Berlin; design Discovery Tours, p. 2/3: Susan Chaaban Dipl.-Des. (FH)
Translated from German by John Sykes, Cologne, Susan Jones, Tübingen, and Suzanne Kirkbright, St Mary Bourne
Editorial office: SAW Communications, Redaktionsbüro Dr. Sabine A. Werner, Mainz: Frauke Feuchter, Julia Gilcher, Cosima Talhouni, Dr. Sabine A. Werner
Prepress: SAW Communications, Mainz, in cooperation with alles mit Medien, Mainz
Phrase book in cooperation with Ernst Klett Sprachen GmbH, Stuttgart, Editorial by Pons Wörterbücher

MIX
Paper from responsible sources
FSC® C124385
www.fsc.org

EXPECTING THAT ZEBRA CROSSINGS ARE SAFE

Not all car or vespa drivers follow the rules and stop at Zebra crossings or red lights. Do what the Italians do: stride confidently across the road, and maintain eye contact with drivers. It's best to cross traffic lanes in the slipstream of Romans who stay alert and find a safe and secure way through the metal jungle.

FLOUTING DRESS CODES

It's well known that visitors to churches are expected to dress decently, which means long trousers for men and no revealing tops for women, for example. Tourists don't have to dress like well-heeled, fashion-conscious Romans, but remember you are not on the beach. Men who leave off their shirts are seen as no better than football hooligans.

SHOW THE MONEY

They look so pleasant, the young girls, who seem to push past you in a packed bus on the way to St Peter's. At the next bus stop, they get off – and unfortunately, often with enough of your money or your mobile phone. Avoid carrying large amounts of cash with you, and leave your passports and jewellery in the hotel safe. Friendly Romans will repeatedly remind you to keep a firm grip of your handbag. Also, remember frequently to change your standing position while on the bus.

BEHAVE DISORDERLY IN ROME

Hooligans have already broken off the trunk of the small marble elephant by Bernini, at night-time the party groups shout and urinate on the Spanish Steps and behave disorderly. Residents in the historic central districts dislike rowdy behaviour. Please respect their *safe zone*!

BUY WATER AT KIOSKS

Fresh spring water was already transported to Rome 2000 years ago using aqueducts. Drinking water still freely flows from the *fontanelle*, the small fountains in the historic centre. At the mobile stands next to major tourist attractions, prices are exorbitant: a small bottle of mineral water or Coca Cola costs 3–4 euros!

DESPAIR ABOUT OPENING HOURS

It's a balmy Roman evening and you're looking forward to a great meal in a recommended little trattoria – and when you get there the shutters are down. No waiter, no chairs on the pavement, no sign about the hours. But don't let the opening hours in Rome drive you to despair! Perhaps it is August, and the owner is relaxing by the sea. Many restaurants in the historic centre work by the mottos "never on a Sunday" and "preferably not on Monday either". Small family-run businesses are especially prone to interruptions if the daughter has her first communion or grandmother dies. Don't begrudge the owner his improvised break: you'll find a good alternative along the street.